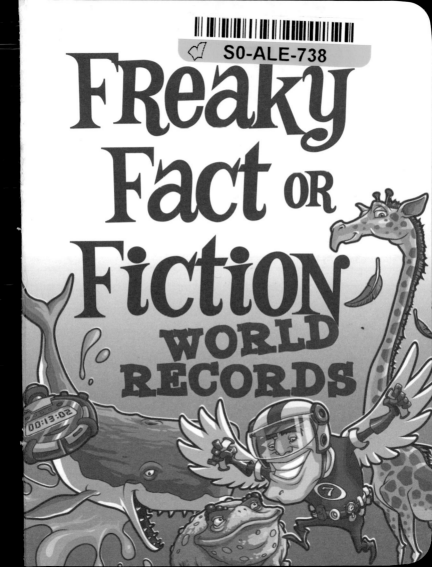

Freaky Fact OR Fiction

WORLD RECORDS

Published by Hinkler Books Pty Ltd
45–55 Fairchild Street
Heatherton Victoria 3202 Australia
www.hinkler.com.au

Author: Dianne Bates
Editor: Suzannah Pearce
Copyeditors: Helena Newton and Susie Ashworth
Design: Diana Vlad and Ruth Comey
Cover Illustration: Rob Kiely
Illustrations: Brijbasi Art Press Ltd
Typesetting: MPS Limited
Prepress: Splitting Image

ISBN: 978 1 7418 5253 0

Printed and bound in China

Freaky Fact or Fiction

They say that truth is stranger than fiction . . . but can you tell the difference?

This book contains over 200 weird and wonderful world records. Most of these are true, but some are tall tales; it will take an expert to spot the difference.

Quiz yourself, your parents, your little sister or your best friend. You can record your answers by ticking one of the circles at the bottom of each page. Then, to check whether you were right, turn to the answers section at the end of the 'facts'.

For extra fun, we've included our sources at the very end of this book. If you want to read more about world records, or if you just want to double-check a fact that sounds crazy, the sources are a good place to begin your research.

You can start anywhere in the book and read the facts in any order. Whatever you do, get ready for hours of *Freaky Fact or Fiction* fun!

Freaky Fact or Fiction

1 Of course there is only one real Santa. We all know that. But the people of Porto, Portugal's second-largest city, decided to break the world record for the largest gathering of Santa Clauses. In 2008, a total of 14,200 participants dressed as Father Christmas, or Pai Natal as he is known in Portugal. This broke the previous world record of 12,965 Santas in Derry City, Northern Ireland the previous year. Every Santa who took part in the Portuguese parade donated money to buy presents for their city's needy children.

 ✓ FACT OR FICTION

2

When we think of gingerbread, we usually think of Germany. That's because of the German story of Hansel and Gretel who found a gingerbread house – with a wicked witch inside! But the tallest gingerbread man was made in 2009 by an American cook, Dave Bowden. He baked and decorated a gingerbread man that was 7.98 m (26 ft 2 in) tall.

✓ **FACT**   **OR**   **FICTION**

Freaky Fact or Fiction

3 The biggest invertebrate (animal without a backbone) on Earth is the giant squid. The largest giant squid ever found measured 18 m (59 ft) long and weighed nearly 900 kg (1 US t). Giant squid and their cousin, colossal squid, have the largest eyes of all animals. Their eyes are around 25 cm (9.8 in) in diameter. With their huge eyes, these animals can see objects in the dark depths where most other animals cannot see at all.

 ✓ FACT OR FICTION

4

Most people can run from 10 to 30 km/h (6.2 to 18.6 mi/h). So just imagine how fast you'd be if you ran 547.2 km/h (340 mi/h)! The fastest-running beetle in the world runs this equivalent speed for its size. The Australian tiger beetle races along at about 9.2 km/h (5.7 mi/h). This means that every second, it runs its own body length about 170 times. Why does it run so fast? It's chasing its dinner. The next fastest insect in the world is the American cockroach, which is a lot slower at 5.6 km/h (3.5 mi/h).

✓ **FACT**   **OR**   **FICTION**

5

In Australia, some people live underground. The reason for this is to shelter from the intense heat of summer, which ranges from 35°C to 45°C (95°F to 113°F) in the shade. More people live underground in the South Australian town of Coober Pedy than anywhere else in the country – around 4000 of them! It's not just the homes that are underground. Motels, hotels, shops and churches are built underground, too. Coober Pedy is the largest opal-mining area in the world.

 ✓ **FACT** **OR** **FICTION**

6 Californian golfer Adam Eves has invented the world's first tracking system to locate lost golf balls. Eves first smears the golf ball with liver paste and then, if it becomes lost, he calls on his dog Sassy to sniff it out. Eves said, 'I'm very happy with the system so far. Sassy never fails to find the ball, whether it's in a pond or long grass. My next step is to train her not to run away with it.'

✓ **FACT** **OR** **FICTION**

7

West Africa is the home of the world's biggest frog. The goliath frog weighs as much as a newborn human baby. It can be as heavy as 3.2 kg (7 lb). It measures up to 75 cm (29.5 in) long with its legs stretched out. Two-thirds of its body is legs, so you can imagine how far it can jump! Although many people enjoy eating frogs, hunting goliath frogs is now against the law.

 ✓ **FACT** **OR**   **FICTION**

8

The United States has more motor vehicles than any other country in the world. There are more than 200 million registered vehicles – or about one vehicle for every two Americans. There are also millions of trucks, campervans and motorcycles. With so many vehicles on the road, it's no wonder that the average American driver spends about 21 hours a year in traffic jams.

✓ **FACT** **OR** **FICTION**

9 Imagine going underwater 53.8 km (33.4 mi) from one place to another. This is how far you would travel in the world's longest underwater tunnel. It is the Seikan Tunnel, found in Japan. The tunnel runs from Japan's main island – Honshu – to Hokkaido, an island to the north. You can travel through the tunnel by train. Or, if you prefer a faster trip, you can fly between the two islands for about the same price.

 ✓ **FACT**   **OR**   **FICTION**

10

Do you like going to amusement parks? In Ohio, USA, you'll find the one with the most rides. Cedar Point Amusement Park has 75 rides for visitors to enjoy. Among the rides is the Skyhawk – the tallest swing ride in the world – and the Top Thrill Dragster roller-coaster – one of the tallest in the world. Altogether, there are 17 roller-coasters. Opened in 1870, Cedar Point has more rides than Disneyland in California, USA.

✓ **FACT** **OR** **FICTION**

11

When Mosha, a baby elephant, stepped on a landmine in 2006, sadly she became an amputee. Later she became the first elephant in the world to be fitted with an adjustable false (prosthetic) leg. Motala, another elephant from Thailand, stepped on a landmine in 1999. This is how she lost her front left leg. Thirty vets worked together to save her life, and in 2009 she was fitted with a new leg made out of silicon and fibreglass. Of course these prosthetic legs are very strong because elephants are very heavy!

 FACT **OR** **FICTION**

12

If you think your local shopping mall is big, think again. The world's largest mall – in Dongguan City, China – is an amazing 600,000 m² (6.5 million ft²) big. Shoppers who don't like walking can travel from place to place by gondolas or water taxis. These go along the 1600 m (1 mi) human-made canal that circles the megamall. Opened in 2005, the mall has seven major areas that resemble cities such as Venice, Amsterdam and Paris.

 FACT **OR** **FICTION**

13

Believe it or not, patê is a food made from goose liver. It was named after a man named Pat Stouffer who was the world's oldest goose breeder in France when he invented the dish in 1633. Every year, the people of his local area, Provence, have a patê festival. Here all the patê makers compete to see whose patê tastes the best. The 2010 winner was Pat Stouffer's great-great-great-great-great-grandson.

✓ **FACT**   **OR**   **FICTION**

14

How many students are there in your school? Only hundreds? Imagine going to a school with 32,114 students! The City Montessori School in Lucknow, India, had that many enrolled in February 2008. This made it the world's largest private school in a single city. How would you find your friends at lunchtime among so many students?

✓ **FACT**   **OR**   **FICTION**

15

If you enjoy playing video games, you probably know the world's best-selling game. It's Wii Sports, a video game that includes sports such as baseball, bowling, tennis, boxing and golf. Created by Japanese Katsuya Eguchi and developed by Nintendo, the game was launched in the USA in 2006 and knocked the 'classic' game Super Mario Bros from the top spot.

 ✓ **FACT** **OR** **FICTION**

16

How many candles on your last birthday cake? Surely not 900. This was the world record for the number of candles on a cake in 1998, but the record has since been broken several times. In 2008, Ashrita Furman set a new world record with a team of over 200 helpers in New York, USA, by lighting 48,523 candles to burn at the same time on a huge cake. The cake was 15.8 × 5.2 m (52 × 17 ft). Eighty helpers used blowtorches to light the candles in just two minutes.

 FACT **OR** **FICTION**

17

Having your body tattooed is a long and painful process. New Zealander Lucky Diamond Rich has spent over 1000 hours having his body tattooed with colourful designs. When nearly all of his body was covered, he decided to have black ink tattoos on every single part of himself. This included his eyelids, the skin between his toes, his gums and even inside his ears. Now Lucky is being tattooed with white designs on top of all his black tattoos. He claims to be the most tattooed person in the world.

 FACT **OR** **FICTION**

18

The world record for people eaten by sharks is 187 in one year. This was in 2001, with most of the people – 97 – taken in the Indian Ocean off the coast of Indonesia and Australia. Shark experts say that warmer waters and increased levels of greenhouse gases were largely to blame. Another factor is an over-population of sharks, again due to warmer ocean waters.

✓ **FACT** **OR** **FICTION**

19

H ave you ever thought of measuring how long your tongue is? According to Guinness World Records, Stephen Taylor from the UK set the record for the longest tongue in 2009. His tongue measured 9.8 cm (3.9 in) from the tip to the middle of his closed top lip. Doesn't that make you want to measure your own tongue?

 ✓ **FACT** OR **FICTION**

20

Jimmy Ferguson is a greedy boy. In 2008, this English child from Hull entered the world record books when he ate 102 cherries in one minute. Although he broke the earlier record of 58 cherries, Jimmy was almost disqualified when he swallowed three cherry stones. However, the judges agreed that the record could stand. Three months later Jimmy entered – but failed to qualify for – an apple-pie-eating competition.

✓ FACT OR FICTION

Freaky Fact or Fiction •••••••••••

21

Garry Turner, of England, has a rare medical condition that affects his skin. But he's turned this to his advantage and set world records. In 1999, Garry stretched the skin of his stomach to an incredible length of 15.8 cm (6.2 in). Garry also has another skin-stretching record. In 2004, he pegged 159 ordinary wooden pegs to every part of his face. His previous record for this was 154 pegs. Can you imagine how much it must have hurt his skin?

 ✓ **FACT** **OR** **FICTION**

22

The tallest man in recorded medical history was Robert Pershing Wadlow who was born in Illinois, USA, in 1918. At his tallest he was 2.72 m (8 ft 11.1 in). His hands measured 32.4 cm (12.75 in) from the wrist to the tip of the middle finger. His heaviest weight – on his 21st birthday – was 222.71 kg (35 st 1 lb).

Robert's father Harold, who was later mayor of Alton, weighed 77 kg (12 st 2 lb). At the age of nine, Robert could carry his father up the stairs of their home.

 FACT **OR** **FICTION**

23

The South American batfish is a species of flying fish found off the waters of Brazil. A small fish, not usually more than about 30 cm (11.8 in) long, it is a poor swimmer but an excellent flyer. Unlike other flying fish, which glide above the water for a short time, the batfish uses its strong bat-like fins to fly great distances, often at speeds of up to 70 km/h (43.5 mi/h). It is thought to be nocturnal.

✓ **FACT** **OR** **FICTION**

24

The World Gurning Championships are held at the Egremont Crab Apple Fair in Cumbria, UK. This event has been running since 1267 and is known around the world. Gurning is another word for 'ugly face'. Competitors don't have to be ugly, but they have to pull the ugliest face in order to win. Tommy Mattinson is the only gurner to have won the World Championship 11 times. His father, Gordon, was the former record holder, winning ten gurning championships.

✓ **FACT** **OR** **FICTION**

25

Most people have only ten fingers (good for adding up!) and ten toes. But two Indians hold the world record for the most fingers and toes. The youngest is Pranamya Menaria, who was born in 2005. He shares the record with Devendra Harne, who was born in 1995. Pranamya and Devendra both have 12 fingers and 13 toes – a total of 25 digits. Their extra digits are the result of a rare medical condition.

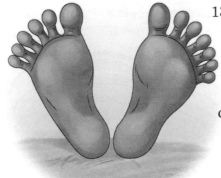

✓ **FACT** **OR** **FICTION**

26

If you ever complain about your brothers and sisters, imagine being one of 19 children! Americans Michelle and Jim Bob Duggar are the proud parents of nine daughters and ten sons. All the children have names starting with 'J', including Jason, James, Justin, Jackson, Johannah and the twins Jedidiah and Jeremiah. In what is claimed to be the world's biggest family, all the children are home-schooled and help with the chores around the house. Wonder who tells the bedtime stories?

✓ **FACT**   **OR**   **FICTION**

27

Australia's Northern Territory is said to be the Crocodile Capital of the World. Crocs are so plentiful there that many locals keep them as pets. In fact, Darwin Council recently introduced a law stating that all crocodiles must be muzzled in public places. Crocodile trainer Lefty Wright is an outspoken critic of this policy. 'There is no need to muzzle crocodiles,' said Mr Wright, who has only one arm and one leg. 'They hardly ever bite, and when they do it's just in fun.'

 ✓ **FACT** **OR** **FICTION**

28

How scary is this? And would you dare to do the same? Would you hold ten live rattlesnakes in your mouth by their tails without any help? This record was set in 2006 by probably the world's bravest (or craziest) man, American Jackie Bibby, known as The Texas Snake Man. Jack also sat in a bathtub with 87 snakes for 45 minutes in 2007.

✓ **FACT** **OR** **FICTION**

The youngest person to ever win an Oscar Award for Best Supporting Actress was American Tatum O'Neal for her role in the movie *Paper Moon* (1973). Tatum, the daughter of Hollywood actor Ryan O'Neal, was only ten when she won the award. The second youngest was New Zealander Anna Paquin, who was 11 when she received her Oscar for her role in *The Piano* (1993). Anna's only previous acting experience was playing a skunk in a school play!

 FACT **OR**   **FICTION**

30

Neighbours, a television show seen around the world, is Australia's longest-running soapie. But it almost wasn't. It went to air in 1985 but it was cancelled by its TV network after only 171 episodes. Happily, another channel picked it up and it went on to show more than 5000 episodes. In Britain, it was the first soapie to be screened twice a day, five days a week. Singer Kylie Minogue was one of its early stars.

 FACT **OR** **FICTION**

Freaky Fact or Fiction

31 One of India's cricketing legends is Sachin Tendulkar, who holds the record for the most runs in a career. His current total of 13,837 runs puts him ahead of Australia's Ricky Ponting (12,026) and West Indian Brian Lara (11,953). A cricket pitch is roughly 20 m (65 ft) long which means Sachin has run over 2767 km (1719 mi) in his career. He must be tired!

✓ FACT OR FICTION

32 Louise Sauvage is one of Australia's top athletes, and she rides to victory in a wheelchair. She has been world number one in her sport of wheelchair track racing a number of times. In Barcelona, Spain, in 1992, Louise competed in her first Paralympics. There she won three gold medals and one silver medal. She has also won a total of six gold medals and three silver medals at the Atlanta, Sydney and Athens Paralympics.

✓ **FACT**   **OR**   **FICTION**

33 **M**rs Gertrude Nutting has been officially named Most Married Woman in the World. First wed at 18, Mrs Nutting, now 96, has been married 27 times. In a bizarre coincidence, her first 26 husbands all died from mushroom poisoning. Her 27th husband, Nick Nutting, died from gunshot wounds, because he wouldn't eat the mushrooms.

Mrs Nutting is now in Middleton Prison, where she works in the kitchen.

 ✓ FACT **OR**   **FICTION**

34

Which of these two cities do you think has the most skyscrapers: New York or Hong Kong? If you said Hong Kong, you were right. A total of 199 skyscrapers tower above the Asian city's streets, slightly more than New York. Because the city has limited land suitable for building, architects must design buildings that use the least amount of land possible. Imagine cleaning all those windows!

✓ FACT OR FICTION

35

The world's slowest swimming fish is actually a horse. A seahorse. These cute little animals range in size from 1.5 cm (0.6 in) to 35 cm (13.8 in). They swim along at 0.3 m (1 ft) every five minutes. That would be 3.3 m (11 ft) every hour. Seahorses propel themselves through the water using a small fin on their backs. This fin flutters up to 35 times per second.

 ✓ **FACT** **OR** **FICTION**

36 A giraffe's neck is 18 times longer than a human's. In fact, giraffes are so tall they hold the record for the world's tallest land mammal. Their necks enable them to reach into high trees for food. Amazingly though, both giraffes and humans have exactly the same number of bones in their necks!

✓ **FACT** **OR** **FICTION**

37

When Audrey Amos was eight years old, she decided to run away from home because her mother would not allow her to wear make-up. The English girl snuck into the backyard of a neighbour who was on holiday. There she climbed a tall tree. When Audrey had climbed as high as she could, she changed her mind.

However, Audrey panicked and could not face the climb down. She yelled for someone to rescue her, but no-one came then, or for the next 39 hours. Thus, Audrey broke the world record for being the youngest person in the world to stay in a tree for more than 30 hours.

 ✓ **FACT**   **OR**   **FICTION**

38

Can you guess the world's slowest land mammal? It's probably not too difficult because lazy people are often said to be slothful. While travelling on land, a three-toed sloth can reach a maximum speed of only 0.11 km/h (0.07 mi/h). If it tried to cross a four-lane street, it would take it almost one quarter of an hour. Sloths find it difficult to walk because of their long claws. As a result, they spend most of their time hanging in trees.

✓ **FACT**   **OR**   **FICTION**

Freaky Fact or Fiction

39

Two hundred people. That's how many could be killed by a single shot of venom from the black mamba. This African reptile is the world's deadliest snake. If not treated straight away, a black mamba's bite can kill. A member of the cobra snake family, the mamba grows to about 4.5 m (14.8 ft) long. If threatened, it lifts its body off the ground and spreads its hood. It then strikes its prey again and again with its long front fangs. So take care if you are wandering around rocky hills or savannas in Africa!

 FACT **OR** **FICTION**

40

Have you ever blown a really big bubble with bubble gum? The Guinness World Record holder for blowing the biggest bubblegum bubble from her nose (where else?) is American grandmother, Joyce Samuels. After inventing this new way to blow a bubble, Joyce broke the world record with a 28 cm (11 in) bubble. She has broken the record again with a 40.6 cm (16 in) bubble blown on a television show. She still holds the current world record.

✓ **FACT** **OR** **FICTION**

41

A world record that has stood since 1891 is the longest distance walked on stilts. In 1891, a French baker named Sylvain Dornon began stilt-walking from Paris, the capital of France, to Moscow, the capital of Russia. It took him 58 days and he walked 2945 km (1830 mi). It is said that he even climbed the Eiffel Tower on his stilts!

 ✓ FACT OR FICTION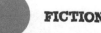

42

Nur Malena Hassan of Malaysia calls herself the Scorpion Queen. For 32 days she lived in a glass container in a shopping centre with 6069 poisonous scorpions. She did this in 2004 to help celebrate her 27th birthday and to reclaim the world record she'd set in 2001 for the longest stay with scorpions. She was only stung seven times but is now the world champion!

 ✓ **FACT** **OR** **FICTION**

Freaky Fact or Fiction

43 American Edwin Sugob has invented the first environmentally friendly multi-purpose gun. Called the Enviro-nator, the weapon fires shotgun-like pellets made from the shells of free-range hens. The Enviro-nator humanely kills cockroaches, wasps, large flies and other household pests. With the press of a button, the remains are vacuumed up into the base of the gun, where they are organically reprogrammed for use as lipstick and suntan lotion.

 ✓ FACT   OR   FICTION

44

In 2007, Russian Olga Dubiousky set a new world record for Pole sitting. Ms Dubiousky sat on the Pole for 182 days. She told reporters that she had not even been thinking about breaking records at the time. 'I was just angry because Thaddeus owed me money and he wouldn't pay it. So I sat on him.' Thaddeus Lutz, the Pole Ms Dubiousky sat on, is expected to make a full recovery.

✓ **FACT**   **OR**   **FICTION**

45 There are many reptiles in the world, such as lizards, snakes, crocodiles and alligators. But the world's largest is the saltwater crocodile, found throughout the East Indies and Australia. These can grow to more than 6.7 m (22 ft) long, twice as long as a car! Large adult saltwater crocodiles may feed on cattle, wild pigs, monkeys and other large mammals. Also known as the Indo-Pacific crocodile and the estuary crocodile, saltwater crocodiles are sometimes found in fresh water.

 ✓ FACT OR FICTION

46

You've often heard of people being lost in the desert and dying of thirst. But do you know which is the world's largest non-polar desert? It's the Sahara Desert, so big that it stretches through ten African countries or 8372 km (5202 mi). The Sahara gets less than 20 cm (7.9 in) of rain a year, which is very little. Oases, or fertile areas that are usually close to a source of water, can be found in the Sahara. Here you will find vegetation such as date palms and acacia trees.

 FACT **OR** **FICTION**

47

Kim Goodman of the USA is able to pop her eyeballs out of her eye sockets a long way. She is said to be able to eye-pop further than anyone in the world. Imagine being able to protrude your eyes out 12 mm (0.47 in) beyond your eye sockets! Kim's eyes were measured doing this in 2007.

 ✓ **FACT** **OR** **FICTION**

48 **K**nown as the stinking corpse lily, the world's largest flower is the rafflesia. An endangered plant, it is found only in the rainforests of Sumatra and Borneo. The blossoms of the rafflesia can weigh up to 11 kg (24 lb 4 oz). The plant lives inside the bark of vines. When it blossoms, the flowers smell like rotten meat. This attracts insects, which help to spread the rafflesia's pollen.

✓ **FACT** **OR** **FICTION**

49

The world's largest leaves are used for weaving baskets and mats. They are from the raffia palm, a native of Madagascar, an island near the coast of Africa. The raffia palm tree has leaves that reach almost 20 m (65.6 ft), just under half the length of an Olympic swimming pool. As well as raffia, other products that come from these palms are floor and shoe polish.

 FACT OR FICTION

50 In Connecticut, USA, two would-be robbers called a bank ahead of time to tell them to get the money ready. Albert Bailey and an unidentified 16-year-old boy turned up (ten minutes later) at the People's United Bank in March 2010. And guess what – they were arrested! There is no official world record, but surely these are the world's most stupid criminals.

✓ **FACT**   **OR**   **FICTION**

Freaky Fact or Fiction

51

Do you think you live in a clean country? In 2010, researchers at US universities Yale and Columbia decided to find out which are the cleanest countries in the world. They looked at factors such as greenhouse emissions, water and air quality, and how a country's environment affected people's health. Although it experienced a volcanic explosion in 2010, which closed flights across northern Europe, Iceland was rated the cleanest country in the world. Bottom of the list of clean countries was Sierra Leone in Africa.

 ✓ FACT **OR** **FICTION**

52

The pygmy sperm whale, at 3.5 m (11 ft) is one of the world's smallest whales. However, the fossil remains of a much smaller whale have recently been found in Peru. The new species, which is about the size of a domestic cat, is called the tiny spotted whale. Its scientific name is *Amberlarus whalari*. Roughly translated from the Latin origin, this means 'traffic light whale'. It is so named because it was covered in bright orange spots, which flashed when it was alarmed.

✓ **FACT** **OR** **FICTION**

53

Adored when he was alive, American singer Elvis Presley still has millions of fans. Known as the King of Rock and Roll, Elvis has sold over one billion records worldwide, more than anyone in record industry history. In America alone, Elvis has had 150 different albums and singles that have been certified gold, platinum or multi-platinum by the Recording Industry Association of America (RIAA).

✓ **FACT** **OR** **FICTION**

54 Pulling weeds from the garden can be difficult. But imagine if you had to pull out the tallest weeds in the world! Growing taller than some trees is the giant hogweed. Part of the carrot or parsley family, this hollow-stemmed weed can grow to a height of 6 m (19.7 ft). It was originally brought from Asia to North America because people liked its tiny white flowers. But now it is a garden pest!

 FACT OR FICTION

55

What is your favourite sweet? Chewing gum? All-day suckers? Chocolate? The world's best-selling sweets, M&M's, were invented in 1941. In 1982, M&M's became the first sweets to go into space. The company Mars Incorporated, which makes M&M's, also produces Pedigree and Whiskas pet food! (By the way, did you know that chocolate can be deadly for dogs?)

 ✓ FACT OR FICTION

56

Spanish-born Pablo Picasso was a gifted child artist who grew up to become the most famous artist of the 20th century. By the age of 13, his drawings were so good he was a more accomplished artist than his father, who was an art teacher. He began his painting career at the age of 16. When Pablo died in 1973, his paintings, ceramics and sculptures had made him very wealthy. In fact his work has earned billions of dollars through sales and auctions. Pablo is best known for co-founding the cubist art movement.

✓ FACT   OR   FICTION

Freaky Fact or Fiction

● ● ● ● ● ● ● ● ● ● ●

57

When she was a child, Oprah Winfrey's only friends were farm animals. She gave them parts in plays that she made up. At church, aged three, Oprah first spoke in public. Her whole town in Kosciusko, Mississippi (USA) knew that she was gifted. She became known as 'the little speaker'. As an adult, Oprah is the world's top-paid entertainer. Her television show, named after herself, began in 1984 and is shown all over the world. On the show she educates viewers about all kinds of social issues. Oprah is extremely wealthy but she has donated millions of dollars to charities.

 ✓ **FACT** **OR** **FICTION**

58

Studies at the University of Washington, USA, have shown that Horatio Jones, a five-year-old chimpanzee, has a brain that is as developed as a child of 12. The chimp can play simple tunes on the piano and recorder, and is also competent at memory tasks and some basic computer games. Horatio Jones is fed a strict diet of organically grown bananas flown in daily from Cuba, but will only eat the skins.

 FACT **OR** **FICTION**

Freaky Fact or Fiction

59

It must be nice to have oodles of money to throw around – especially if you are a child. The world's youngest billionaire was left a great fortune by her grandfather, Aristotle Onassis, when he died. When Greek-born Athina Onassis Roussel turned 18 in 2003, she inherited about US$3 billion (A$3.43 billion or £2.07 billion) in properties. (This included her own private jet!) Athina's mother Christina Onassis died when Athina was only three, so she was raised by her father Thierry Roussel and his wife.

 ✓ **FACT**   **OR**   **FICTION**

60

Through his foundation, the world's richest man has donated billions of dollars to charity. American Bill Gates is known to most people because he is the co-founder of Microsoft, said to be the biggest computer software company in the world. It employs more than 78,000 people in 105 countries. Bill became a billionaire in 1986, and for 14 of the past 15 years was ranked as the richest person in the world. Bill's interest in computers started when he was a teenager.

✓ **FACT** **OR**   **FICTION**

61 A little steakhouse in Tokyo, Japan, serves what is probably the world's most expensive first course. The Aragawa restaurant only has one entrée. It is Wagyu (Kobe) beef, made from cows fed on sake (a rice wine) and given massages. Served with pepper and mustard, the beef dish costs around A\$480 (US\$400 or £276)! Despite being so expensive, you have to book well ahead to get into Aragawa, which is Japan's first steakhouse.

✓ **FACT** OR **FICTION**

62

Do you spend much time surfing the web? The country in the world that has the most Internet users is also the country that invented computers. Americans currently make up 17 per cent of users worldwide. More than half of the population of the United States spends about 14 hours online every week. The countries that are searched for most often on Google are Luxembourg and Singapore.

✓ **FACT**   **OR**   **FICTION**

Freaky Fact or Fiction

63

The world's biggest environment group is in Japan. It is made up of over one million people, mostly students who are opposed to environmental threats such as greenhouse gas emissions, timber cutting and coal mining. In 2001, the group known as the Federation of Industrial Litterers, Takers and Hijackers (FILTH) decided to fight against whaling in the Pacific Ocean. However, they were fined six million yen by the Japanese government when they demonstrated in Tokyo.

 ✓ **FACT** **OR** **FICTION**

64

We all know that the sun has the hottest surface in the universe. But do you know the planet with the hottest surface? If you guessed Venus, you're right. Its surface temperature can reach a sizzling 465°C (869°F). That is far hotter than the average temperature where you live! Venus, the planet closest to Earth, is surrounded by acid clouds. Not a nice place to go for your holidays.

 ✓ **FACT**   **OR**   **FICTION**

Freaky Fact or Fiction

65

In the 1930s, the biggest movie star in the world was a little American girl, Shirley Temple. A talented singer and dancer, Shirley started performing soon after she could walk. In Los Angeles, when she was three years old, she starred in a series of films called 'Baby Burlesks'. For this she was paid US$10 a day (around A$12 or £7). Shirley then appeared in a string of films in the early to mid-1930s. In fact, she made 11 films in 1933. When she was six years old and went to see Santa Claus in a department store, Santa asked her for her autograph!

 ✓ FACT **OR** **FICTION**

66

Meet Crabzilla! He's a monster crab with legs longer than a man's. He's so big he measures 3.048 m (10 ft) from claw to claw and is the biggest crab ever seen in Britain. Crabzilla was plucked from the depths of the Pacific Ocean and spent some time at the National Sea Life Centre in Birmingham. Nobody knows how old Crabzilla is, but he is still growing and could live up to 100 years.

 ✓ **FACT**　 **OR**　 **FICTION**

Freaky Fact or Fiction

67

In 1892, Sweden's Frizen Burgher became the first person to open a fast-food restaurant. The early menu was very basic, with only two items listed: Cup of Cabbage (2 öre) or Cabbage Supreme (5 öre). The business was slow to begin with but took off in 1894 when Burgher added sesame seeds to the menu. By 1900, there was a chain of Frizen Burgher restaurants throughout Sweden.

 FACT OR FICTION

68

George and Minnie Sesler, from the USA, had eight children. In the 1920s, the four eldest of their five sons were born with a rare genetic condition called albinism. People with albinism have little or no pigment in their eyes, skin or hair. No matter what their race, their skin is translucent, their hair is white and their eyes are pinkish-blue. A Canadian family shares the title of the most albino siblings. All four of Mario and Angie Gaulin's children were born in the 1980s with an even rarer form of the condition, and Mr Gaulin has the condition too.

✓ FACT   OR   FICTION

Freaky Fact or Fiction

69

 amed Russian novelist Leo Tolstoy (1828–1910) was the inventor of the world's first childproof lock. Tolstoy insisted on privacy when he was writing, but his children always found a way to open the lock on his study door. To overcome this he wired the door so that anyone trying to open the lock would receive a small electric shock. Although the lock proved highly effective, he was unable to sell the idea for commercial use.

 FACT OR FICTION

70

The things some people do to get in the record books! Ken Edwards of Derbyshire, England, ate 36 cockroaches in one minute on the set of *The Big Breakfast* in London, England, in 2001 to set a Guinness World Record. A retired rat-catcher, Ken has also been a part-time entertainer since the age of 18. While munching on his cockroaches Ken said, 'It's like having an anesthaetic at the back of the throat.' This is because cockroaches let off a scent to discourage predators! Yum!

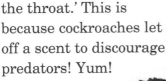

 FACT   **OR**   **FICTION**

71

Cathie Jung's waist is the smallest in the world. About the same size as a regular jar of mayonnaise, it's 38.1 cm (15 in) round. In 1997 Cathie started wearing a corset. She now wears one 24 hours a day to keep herself as slim as can be. The corset queen says she probably has around 100 corsets. Cathie comes from Connecticut, USA, and has her own corset website.

 ✓ FACT OR FICTION

72

Burper King. This is what Englishman Paul Hunn proudly calls himself. On the set of a television show in London in 2008, Paul set the record for the loudest burp in the world. It was 107.1 decibels. Paul says he 'was always known for burping loudly at school'. At 107.1 decibels, Paul's burp was louder than a chainsaw, a lawnmower or a subway train!

 FACT **OR** **FICTION**

Freaky Fact or Fiction

73

Lee Redmond, from the USA, decided she wanted the longest fingernails in the world. So she stopped cutting her nails in 1979. She grew and carefully manicured them. Finally they reached a total length of 8.65 m (28 ft 4.5 in). This record length was measured on the set of *Lo show dei record* in Madrid, Spain in 2008. Lee's longest nail was the right thumbnail at 90 cm (2 ft 11 in). However, in 2009, Lee lost her fingernail record when she was involved in a car accident. She now says, 'Life is a lot easier.'

✓ **FACT** **OR** **FICTION**

74 According to Guinness World Records, the most spoons anyone has balanced on their face is 16. Joe Allison of Devon, UK, achieved this feat using stainless steel teaspoons in 2008. Joe balanced five spoons on his forehead, four on his cheeks, one on his nose, two on his top lip, one on each ear and two on his chin. Now don't you want to go and practise to beat his record?

✓ **FACT**   **OR**   **FICTION**

Freaky Fact or Fiction

75

In September 2008, Phyllis and Ralph Tarrant of Sheffield, UK, had a combined age of 205. Ralph, 105, and his wife claimed the title of Britain's oldest couple when Phyllis turned 100. They married in 1933. They said that their old age was due to 'getting on with each other, a good diet, exercise [and] avoiding cigarettes'.

✓ **FACT**   **OR**   **FICTION**

76

Norwegian Iral Rail is credited with having the most rapid growth spurt in human history by the World Medical Statistics Centre in Paris, France. Rail was a 14-year-old jockey who, in 1972, was riding in a 3.2 km (2 mi) horse race. At the start of the race he was 152 cm (5 ft) tall, but turning for home he experienced a dramatic growth spurt. At the finish he had shot up to 182.9 cm (6 ft). Rail's mount won the race but was later disqualified, because Rail's feet had touched the ground.

 FACT **OR** **FICTION**

77

Charin Yuthasastrkosol was born in Thailand in 1930 and now lives in the USA. At the age of 47, she began ballet lessons and has not stopped dancing since. In 2002, she held the world record for being the oldest ballet dancer in the world. Charin performs regularly at galas, one of her most notable being a performance for Thailand's Ambassador to the USA in New Mexico, USA, when she was 71 years and 203 days old.

 FACT **OR** **FICTION**

78

Imagine reading aloud for ten straight days! This is what six American women did in 2009 to set a new world record for 'Longest Reading Aloud Marathon by a Team'. The women, from the International Solidarity for Human Rights organisation, read the 30 Articles of the Universal Declaration of Human Rights repeatedly at a campus of Miami Dade College in Little Havana, USA.

✓ **FACT** **OR** **FICTION**

79

The world's strangest outside toilet must surely be that used by astronauts Neil Armstrong, Michael Collins and Edwin 'Buzz' Aldrin. In 1969, these men made up the crew aboard *Apollo 11*, the rocket that made the first Moon landing. Its designers insisted that *Apollo 11* should be as light as possible to allow it to break free of Earth's gravitational force. Because of this, *Apollo 11* was small and cramped. The astronauts were fitted with a harness and lowered out of the escape hatch when they needed to go to the toilet.

 FACT **OR** **FICTION**

80

Which do you think is our planet's largest ocean? It's the Pacific, which is not only Earth's largest ocean but also the world's largest and deepest body of water. It makes up nearly 46 per cent of all the water in the world's oceans. And its average depth is more than 4200 m (more than 14,000 ft). All the land on Earth, plus a bit more, could fit into the Pacific Ocean.

✓ **FACT**   **OR**   **FICTION**

81

Sometimes rich people can do a lot to help our planet. In 2007, British businessman Sir Richard Branson decided to award an 'Earth Challenge' prize. The award of US$25 million (A$29.5 million or £17.3 million) was the largest environmental award in the world. It is to be awarded to the person or group that provides the best solution to removing carbon dioxide from the Earth's atmosphere.

 FACT **OR** **FICTION**

82

So you thought last winter was cold? You don't know cold! The lowest temperature ever recorded on Earth was –89.2°C (–128.6°F) in 1983. The place was Vostok Station in Antarctica. The Russian research station at Vostok is operated by scientists from all over the world, including US, French and Russian – all of them very cold!

 ✓ **FACT** **OR** **FICTION**

83

Imagine a bird that dives under water and stays there for a long time! At sea, emperor penguins can dive deeper than any other bird. They can dive to 565 m (1850 ft) and stay under for more than 20 minutes. These incredible birds have many layers of air, skin and blubber to help keep out the sub-zero temperatures. And they have the highest density of feathers of all bird species. On land, penguins huddle to stay warm. Once a penguin feels warmer it will move to the edge of the group so that others can have a turn at being protected from the harsh elements.

 ✓ **FACT** **OR** **FICTION**

84

They are no bigger than a human hand, or the size of a sparrow. That's the size of the world's smallest owls. They are the elf owl from southwestern USA and Mexico, and the least pygmy owl of Brazil, Argentina and Paraguay. The smallest owls are around 13 cm (5.1 in) tall and weigh less than 50 g (1.75 oz).

✓ **FACT** **OR** **FICTION**

Freaky Fact or Fiction

85 Look! Up in the air! It's a bird! It's a plane! No, it's DC's *Action Comics #1*, the world's most expensive comic book! Published in 1938, this title marks the first appearance of Superman. One of these comics sold at auction in 2006 for US$195,000 (A$230,000 or £134,800), US$70,000 (A$82,600 or £48,400) more than a copy of *Amazing Fantasy #15*, which contained the first appearance of Spider-Man. The reason that the first Superman comic is so valuable is that it marked the first time a superhero of any kind appeared in the fiction world.

 FACT OR FICTION

86

Danish adventurer Unli Kely was the first woman to cross Australia's Nullarbor Plain by pogo stick. The crossing took 19 days. For much of that time the temperature was more than 45°C (113°F). Ms Kely made the journey to honour the kangaroo, which was the inspiration for the pogo stick. Asked to describe her experience, she said, 'It had its ups and downs.'

 FACT **OR** **FICTION**

87

an you guess the smelliest animal in the world? No, not your little brother! It is in fact the striped skunk, which lives in North America. When threatened, the skunk squirts a truly stinky liquid from a gland under its tail. The stench is so strong that people could smell it if a teaspoonful was tipped into a full-length swimming pool! But luckily, it doesn't harm you – except to make you bad company for at least a week until the smell begins to fade.

✓ FACT OR FICTION

88

Also known as a dwarf monkey, the pygmy marmoset is the smallest true monkey in the world. It can fit into a human palm and it's body can be so small it is only as long as an adult human's thumb. It grows to a height of about 12.7 cm (5 in), not including its tail, and weighs up to 199 g (7 oz). The pygmy marmoset has hair on its head that looks a bit like a mane. It is a tree-dweller that lives in dense forests in the Upper Amazon basin in countries such as Brazil, Ecuador and Peru.

 FACT **OR** **FICTION**

89

The world's biggest table-tennis club is in China. It is made up of over one million people, mostly students. Members take table tennis very seriously, with many practising for up to six hours a day. Club President Lee Ping Pongii said that table tennis is faster than tennis and squash, and requires greater mental effort than chess. He believes that Albert Einstein might have achieved more success in science if not for the fact that he was a keen table-tennis player. 'After a few games his mind was exhausted,' Lee Ping Pongii explained.

 FACT **OR**   **FICTION**

90

The titan beetle of the Amazon rainforest is the longest beetle without horns in the world. Full-grown adults can grow up to 16.5 cm (6.5 in) long – as big as an adult human's handspan. The beetle is also very heavy even though it does not feed (it only lives for a few weeks). It simply flies around in search of a mate. Its mandibles are strong enough to snap a pencil in two.

✓ **FACT** **OR** **FICTION**

91

The heaviest and tallest bird in the world is the ostrich. It also has the largest eye of any land animal, measuring almost 5 cm (2 in) across. A flightless bird, the ostrich lives in African savanna and desert lands. It is a strong runner and races along at up to 70 km/h (43 mi/h). Its powerful, long legs can cover 3 to 5 m (9.8 to 16.4 ft) in a single step. An ostrich's kick is so strong it can kill a human. It has a long, sharp claw on each two-toed foot.

 ✓ FACT OR FICTION

92 Although it is the longest reptile in the world, the reticulated python is not poisonous. Found throughout South-East Asia, this giant reptile's average length is 3 to 6.1 m (10 to 20 ft). The longest python ever recorded was in Indonesia in 1912 – a monster at around 10 m (32.8 ft) long. Reticulated pythons eat warm-blooded prey, from birds to humans, depending on how big the snake is. They live for about 20 years.

✓ **FACT**   **OR**   **FICTION**

Freaky Fact or Fiction

93

The world's deepest hole is said to be in Mexico. At over 30 km (18.6 mi) deep, it is located near the country's capital, Mexico City. As wide as ten freeways, the hole is on the site of the ancient city of Mexikaka. For centuries, looters have dug ever deeper into the hole to search for lost treasure. In an effort to fill it, officials now encourage residents to tip their rubbish into the hole: old cars, furniture, plastic bags, everything! It is estimated that it will take another 200 years to fill.

✓ **FACT** **OR** **FICTION**

94

Imagine a snail that stretches from your mum's wrist to her elbow. That's the average length of the world's largest snail, the giant African land snail. These enormous creatures reproduce quickly, laying as many as 100 to 400 eggs at a time. A Miami boy smuggled three giant African land snails into the USA in 1966. They were released into a garden, and in seven years, there were more than 18,000 snails. The snail has also become a huge nuisance in Brazil, where they were once imported as food.

 ✓ **FACT**   **OR**   **FICTION**

Freaky Fact or Fiction

Any guess as to which is the world's sleepiest marsupial? Yes, it's the koala. Sometimes called 'a bear' (though it's not), the koala mostly eats the leaves of eucalyptus trees. It then sleeps up to 18 hours out of every 24. Koalas eat so many eucalyptus leaves that they smell like cough drops. When not asleep, a koala feeds, mostly at night. Koalas do not drink much water. They get most of their moisture from leaves.

✓ FACT OR FICTION

96

Carnivores are meat-eaters. The largest of all land carnivores is the polar bear. The weight of an adult male averages 400 to 600 kg (880 to 1320 lb), which is really heavy! From nose to tail, they measure around 2.4 to 2.6 m (7.9 to 8.5 ft), which is taller than a man. Polar bears also have the most sensitive noses of all land animals. They could smell you if you were more than 30 km (18 mi) away! They eat animals such as seals, walruses and whales, and are very strong swimmers.

✓ **FACT** **OR** **FICTION**

97 Australians Tilly and Theresa Flower were born on the same day, 20 March 1906, in Fairfield, New South Wales. They are the world's oldest twins. Neither woman has ever married. And both have lived together since they left home at the age of 21. Both worked as nurses. They have always dressed alike. Tilly and Theresa say they have lived so long because they took up yoga and meditation at the age of 85. They also never smoked or drank. Their only problem is that now they can't remember who is Tilly and who is Theresa.

 ✓ **FACT** **OR** **FICTION**

98

The largest fish in the sea is the whale shark. It can grow to 18 m (59 ft), but usually measures 4 to 12 m (13.1 to 39.4 ft). Scientists used to think that whale sharks laid eggs, but in 1995 a pregnant whale shark was captured. This means that whale sharks probably give birth to live young. Whale sharks' favourite meal is plankton. They scoop these tiny plants and animals into their huge mouths while swimming close to the surface. They also eat small fish. Although they are huge, whale sharks are actually quite gentle and not dangerous to humans.

✓ **FACT** **OR** **FICTION**

Freaky Fact or Fiction

99

The ten tallest mountains in the world are found in the Himalayan mountain range, and the 50 tallest mountains in the world are all found in Asia. But the highest mountain in the world – in the Himalayas, between China and Nepal – is Mount Everest. It is 8850 m (29,035 ft) tall. Formed about 60 million years ago, Mount Everest was first climbed in 1953 by New Zealander Sir Edmund Hillary and Nepalese Tenzing Norgay.

 ✓ FACT **OR** **FICTION**

100

In 2010, Britain created the world's biggest marine reserve. The 545,000 km² (210,000 mi²) reserve is around the Chagos Islands in the Indian Ocean. The archipelago is considered to be one of the world's richest marine ecosystems. Experts say it compares to Australia's Great Barrier Reef for its marine life. It will include a reef where commercial fishing will be banned. The Chagos Islands were ceded (given up) to Britain in 1814.

✓ **FACT** **OR** **FICTION**

Freaky Fact or Fiction

101

Bunny and Big Bob Smith of Liverpool, England, have been voted the World's Messiest Couple. However, they have also proven that being messy can be a good thing. When a TV news crew drove past their house in August 2010, they were shocked by what they saw. 'The mess was incredible,' said a reporter. 'It looked like a hurricane had hit'. The crew called for emergency services to attend. Soon after, a hurricane did actually arrive. Many lives were saved because they received prompt medical treatment. It was later found that the Smiths' house always looked like it had been hit by a hurricane.

✓ **FACT** **OR** **FICTION**

102

Is this the world's meanest woman? In 2010, an American woman was found guilty of swapping two children for US$175 (A$206 or £120) and a cockatoo. Donna Louise Greenwell received 15 months of hard labour on each charge. She was accused of selling a couple a four-year-old girl and a five-year-old boy. The children's parents had left both children in Greenwell's care.

 ✓ **FACT** **OR** **FICTION**

Freaky Fact or Fiction

103

French Spider-Man. That's what they call Alain Robert. Often wearing T-shirts that call attention to environmental issues or appeal for peace, Alain climbs monuments and skyscrapers without any equipment, such as ropes or harnesses. Using window frames, cables and gaps between brickwork, Alain holds the record for scrambling up the most buildings in the world without assistance. He even has a website to let people know which buildings he has climbed.

✓ **FACT** **OR** **FICTION**

104

Denmark has the oldest flag in the world. Called 'the Dannebrog', the Danish flag appears in a Danish text from 1478. And it was in a Dutch text 100 years earlier when it was a red banner with a white cross and a coat of arms. Danish mythology says that the Dannebrog first appeared in the 1200s when it fell from the sky during a battle.

✓ **FACT**   **OR**   **FICTION**

105

There are no letters in written Chinese, only words. Each word has its own symbol, and over 2000 of them are used in everyday speech. Dating back around 7000 years, it is believed to be the oldest written language. Mandarin, spoken by 810 million Chinese, is the most commonly spoken language in the world. Another interesting written language is Hawaiian, with only 12 letters.

 ✓ **FACT** **OR** **FICTION**

106

Mikayla-Lee Gregorivich became the world's greatest plate breaker in May 2010. The 18-year-old waitress set her record at the famous Hotel Spectacular in Moscow, which was hosting a grand dinner for 10,000 people. While carrying a tray of baby snapping turtles, she was bitten on her little finger. In shock, she tripped over a rug and fell into a table holding 5000 dinner plates. Only 50 plates were undamaged, making Gregorivich the new world champion plate breaker! To mark the achievement, Russian Prime Minister Vladimir Putin presented her with the prestigious China-Shop-Bull Award.

 FACT **OR** **FICTION**

107

The Tube, or London Underground rail system, is the world's largest. It is also the oldest public underground railway. The noisy, steam rail system opened on 10 January 1863. Trains ran every ten minutes and tens of thousands of people travelled on the Tube on the first day. Today there are 274 stations along its 408 km (254 mi) of track. There are actually 12 deep bore tunnels that make up the Tube. Over 700 million journeys are made on the Tube every year.

 FACT **OR** **FICTION**

108

China has more people than any other country on Earth. The population is more than 1.3 billion. One person in five alive today resides in China. In 1979, in order to slow down the population growth, the government announced the one-child policy. This meant that couples could only have one child. In spite of this, China's population is expected to reach 1.4 billion by 2015.

✓ **FACT** **OR** **FICTION**

109

Imagine being born with hair covering your face. According to Guinness World Records, a Mexican family of 19 is the hairiest in the world. They are the Ramos Gomez family. Hypertrichosis – or hairiness – is the rare medical condition that accounts for them having so much hair on their bodies. Two of the family members, brothers Larry and Danny, travel around the world to exhibit their hairiness for a living.

✓ **FACT** **OR** **FICTION**

110

The world's most expensive book was written by English writer, William Shakespeare. *First Folio*, a first edition collection of Shakespeare's plays, published in 1623, was sold at auction in 2001 for US$5.2 million (A$5.9 million or £3.5 million). Coming second in the most expensive book category is a first edition of recipes by Napoleon Bonaparte. Written in 1792, *I Came, I Saw, I Ate* sold for £2.5 million (US$3.6 million or A$4.2 million) at auction in 2007.

✓ **FACT**   **OR**   **FICTION**

Freaky Fact or Fiction

111

When she had a motorcycle accident in 2004, Claudia Mitchell's left arm was cut off. However, she was lucky because she became the first woman to be fitted with an artificial arm. Ms Mitchell, a former US Marine Corps officer from Maryland, is able to control parts of her bionic arm by thought. When she feels what she is touching with her bionic hand, it feels as if she is touching it with her own hand. This is because of the work of very clever doctors.

 FACT **OR** **FICTION**

112

Life expectancy refers to how long you are expected to live. In the top 20 countries in the western world, people have a life expectancy of over 80 years. However, the country with the lowest life expectancy is a developing country in Africa. If you lived in Angola, where there is a lot of poverty and disease, you would expect to live only 39 years if you were a man, and 37 years if you were a woman.

✓ **FACT** **OR** **FICTION**

113

When she was only seven years old, American Vivian Wheeler had a hairy face and her father insisted she shave it. Since 1993, Vivian has let her beard grow. This means that at one time she had the longest beard on a woman in the world. When her beard was measured in 2000, from skin to the tip of the longest hair, it measured 27.9 cm (11 in). Being hairy hasn't stopped Vivian from being married: she's been married four times!

 FACT **OR** **FICTION**

114

Engl002nglish girl Montana Jones won the 2011 British National Essay Competition, which was held to find the child who had the best excuse for not doing their homework. In her essay, Montana wrote that she had placed her homework, written on one sheet of folded A4 paper, on her teacher's desk. Later, the teacher put a sandwich on the desk, on top of Montana's homework. At lunchtime she ate the sandwich, not realising that the homework was stuck to it. Montana is probably the only child in the world who can say a teacher ate her homework.

✓ **FACT** **OR** **FICTION**

Freaky Fact or Fiction

115

How happy are you? How happy are the people around you? The World Database of Happiness in the Netherlands conducts surveys to decide which is the happiest country in the world. In 2008, Australia came in at number six, the USA gained 17th place and Great Britain was in 22nd place. The country with the happiest people was Denmark, followed by Switzerland. Denmark has an extensive welfare system, with most of its services (such as education and health care) free. However, its people pay a lot of taxes!

 FACT **OR** **FICTION**

116

When he was seven years old, Indian boy Kishan Shrikanth learnt how orphans and poor children in his country were forced to work for a living. This inspired him to make a movie titled *C/o Footpath* in 2006 at the age of 10. This made Kishan the world's youngest director of a professionally made feature-length movie. It featured top Bollywood stars Jackie Shroff and Saurabh Shukla, and award-winning actress Thaara.

✓ FACT   OR   FICTION

117

The first woman to climb the world's highest mountain, Mount Everest, was from Japan. She is Junko Tabei, who reached the summit in 1975. The first woman to reach the summit of Mount Everest from both the north and south sides was South African Cathy O'Dowd. She conquered the south side in 1996 and the north in 1999.

 FACT **OR** **FICTION**

118

The first time he was struck by lightning, Roy Cleveland Sullivan lost a toenail. After that, his eyebrows were burned, his hair was burned twice and he was burned on other parts of his body. Roy, a US forest ranger in Shenandoah National Park, Virginia, earned the nickname 'Human Lightning Rod'. This was because he was the only person in the world to be hit by lightning seven different times and survive.

✓ **FACT**   **OR**   **FICTION**

119

ost people's hearts are in their chests. But there is a rare medical condition where the heart is not in the right place. American Christopher Wall was born with all the right parts, except that one very important part was in the wrong place. His heart was outside his body. Nobody knows why. The condition is so rare that out of every one million babies born, only about five to eight of them will have the condition known as *Ectopia cordis*. Christopher was born in 1975 and is the longest-known survivor of this condition.

 ✓ FACT OR FICTION

120

The world's hardest puzzle contest is Blind Jigsaw. Players must assemble a jigsaw of not less than 5000 pieces while wearing a blindfold. World Blind Jigsaw Championship organiser Daley Larma said, 'It takes a little to master the technique but, in time, those who play this game learn to see with their fingers.' The first World Championship began in Sweden in 2002. Leading the competition so far is Miles Togo, who has correctly fitted four pieces.

✓ **FACT** **OR** **FICTION**

121

To celebrate his 11th birthday in 2009, American Fin Keheler decided to try to set a new Guinness World Record. He wanted to break the world record for sticking snails to his face. The previous record was 37. Fin said, 'I thought I could totally beat that (record) because I'm not grossed out by snails like most people are.' Helpers had one minute to place as many snails as possible on Fin's face. Then Fin sat up and the snails had to stay on for 10 seconds. On the fourth and final attempt, helpers counted 43!

 ✓ **FACT** **OR** **FICTION**

122

In 2007, Francis Joyon decided to sail solo and non-stop around the world. Now this French sailor holds the world's fastest solo circumnavigation sailing record of 57 days, 13 hours, 34 minutes and six seconds, which he achieved in January 2008. In doing this, he beat the previous record by 14 days, which was held by Dame Ellen MacArthur of the UK.

✓ **FACT**   **OR**   **FICTION**

Freaky Fact or Fiction

123 One of the world's greatest adventurers was Steve Fossett, a balloonist. In his balloon, he was the first person in the world to fly solo across the Pacific Ocean, the first to cross the African continent, the first to cross the European continent and the first to cross the South Atlantic and Indian oceans. He was also the first person to fly a balloon solo around the world. In this last attempt, Steve averaged only four hours of sleep a day, in a sleeping bag. Sadly, in 2007, he went missing while flying a plane in the USA.

✓ FACT OR FICTION

124

Famous English gardener Manny Ure is best known for creating the most unusual hedge in the world. Tired of traditional hedges that need to be constantly trimmed, Ure came up with something very different. In 1856, he made a hedge by placing sculptures of 12 large hogs side-by-side. The idea soon caught on and hog hedges could be seen throughout England. There were also cow and horse hedges, but Ure's design was the most popular. This is where the word 'hedgehog' came from.

 FACT **OR** **FICTION**

Freaky Fact or Fiction

125

Do you like riding your bike? Italian Vittorio Innocente does – but he prefers to cycle underwater. In fact, he holds the world record for deepest underwater cycling. In 2008, Vittorio mounted his bike at a depth of 28 m (92 ft), then rode down a 110 m (360 ft) long underwater slope. Continuing downwards, he broke the previous world record of 60 m (197 ft), which he set himself three years earlier. 'It was tough because I ran into more mud than I expected,' Vittorio said.

 ✓ **FACT** **OR** **FICTION**

126

Barack Hussein Obama II was born on 4 August 1961. He is the 44th and current President of the United States. He is the first African-American to hold this office. When he was a child, Barack was known at home and at school as Barry. He was born in Hawaii but also lived in Indonesia for about five years. When he was in third grade, Barack wrote an essay saying that he wanted to become US president.

✓ **FACT**   **OR**   **FICTION**

127

Imagine going on an Easter-egg hunt for more than half a million eggs! In 2007, over 9000 children went hunting for eggs in the world's largest Easter-egg hunt. The venue was the Cypress Gardens Adventure Park in Florida, USA. Altogether, 501,000 eggs were hidden. Though most were filled with sweets and toys, some contained prizes donated by local businesses. One lucky egg even held a two-year college scholarship.

 ✓ FACT **OR** FICTION

128

At the UK National Giant Vegetable Championships every year, giant vegetables are exhibited. In 2006, the longest cucumber measured 89.2 cm (35.1 in). It was grown by Alfred J Cobb. In 2003, Alfred grew the heaviest cucumber, a beauty at 12.4 kg (27 lb 5 oz). A spokesman for the championships said that a sunny and wet start to the British summer helps growers to set new world records.

✓ FACT   OR   FICTION

129

Radar is certainly one colossal horse! He is featured in the Guinness World Records book as the world's tallest living horse. A Belgian draft horse, he stands over 19 hands high, or 202 cm (79.5 in). He also weighs over 1088.6 kg (2400 lb). Radar, a gelding born in 1998, has a huge appetite. He eats 8.2 kg (18 lb) of grain, 18.1 kg (40 lb) of hay and drinks 75.7 L (20 US gal) of water each day.

✓ **FACT** **OR** **FICTION**

130

Think Rock Paper Scissors is a children's game? Think again. World championships are held every year. Five hundred top players from around the globe gathered in Toronto, Canada, in 2006, to compete for the title of world champion. The winner was a British man, Bob Cooper. The simple game is often used to make decisions. Players smack their fists into their palms and count to three before making one of three hand signals representing different objects: a fist is a rock, a flat hand is paper and two fingers are scissors. Paper covers rock, scissors cut paper and rock breaks scissors.

 FACT **OR** **FICTION**

131

After months of testing, scientists have officially named Australia's James Fogh as the world's most forgetful man. They say Fogh does not have any diseases of the brain; he is just extremely absent-minded. During the tests Fogh, a primary school principal, frequently forgot his own name, his wife's name and where they lived. He also forgot to eat and to bathe. Once while teaching a class, he forgot that anyone else was there, and made a very rude noise. His condition improved after treatment, which included lengthy sessions of running on the spot. This was to jog his memory.

 FACT **OR** **FICTION**

132

Some people enjoy dressing up as animals. They are called furries and there is even a fan website called Cool Furries. Furry fandom began during the 1980s as a mix of science fiction, comic book and animation fans. It has fans all over the world. The largest annual furry gathering is at the Anthrocon convention in the USA. At the 2010 convention, 4238 furries attended.

✓ **FACT** **OR** **FICTION**

Freaky Fact or Fiction

133

Thousands of holy men smeared with ash plunge into the sacred waters of the Ganges River every three years. They are celebrating Kumbh Mela, a Hindu spiritual festival. It is considered to be the world's largest religious gathering. The pilgrimage rotates between four different locations in India. In 2010, the Kumbh Mela, or Pitcher Festival, was expected to attract over 50 million pilgrims. The Kumbh Mela got its name from a mythical fight over a pitcher of holy nectar. Gods and demons waged a war over the nectar needed to achieve immortality and victory.

 ✓ FACT OR FICTION

134 Anyone wanting to counterfeit (or copy) Swiss money has a very difficult job. Swiss franc notes are said to be the most secure banknotes in the world. Copying them is almost impossible because they have 18 security features. For one, the note paper is made from the by-products of cotton-making. The notes are printed using special inks. The text on them is so tiny it can only be read with a magnifying glass. And like Australian banknotes, they are machine-washable at high temperatures.

✓ FACT   OR   FICTION

Freaky Fact or Fiction •••••••••••

135

The youngest self-made millionaire in history was Jackie Coogan. Born in Los Angeles, California, Jackie began his acting career as an infant in a film, *Skinner's Baby*. His first theatre performance was at age four. As a child Jackie toured with his family in vaudeville shows. And he was chosen by actor Charlie Chaplin to star with him in the movie *The Kid*. By 1923, at age 9, Jackie was one of the highest paid stars in Hollywood. At that time he was earning US $22,000 (A$25,145 or £11,936) per week.

✓ **FACT** **OR** **FICTION**

136

It's official: the world's smartest person is nine-year-old Japanese girl, Iso Hokay. At the age of three Iso taught her own parents to read! By five she had passed a university entrance exam, and by seven she had completed a master's degree. She is now a Professor of Mangaology. (Mangaology is the scientific study of Manga comics). Scientists believe Iso owes her incredible intelligence to her diet. Since she was a baby she has eaten nothing but raw fish.

 ✓ **FACT** **OR**   **FICTION**

Freaky Fact or Fiction

137

The highest selling painting by a wild animal was made by Koma, a white rhinoceros from South Africa. Landscape painter Günter Volk had just set up his easel and canvas for a day's sketching, when Koma charged. Volk climbed a tree to escape and stayed there for five hours. Meanwhile, the enraged Koma tramped up and down on the wet canvas, spreading paint everywhere. Back on the ground and safe, Volk was amazed at what the rhino had produced. He sold the painting at auction in 2009 for US$340,000 (A$400,000 or £234,000). All efforts to get Koma to paint again have failed.

 FACT **OR** **FICTION**

138

ony Blair is the Labour Party's longest continuously serving British prime minister. When he was elected as leader of the British Labour Party in 1994, he was also its youngest-ever head. Mr Blair served as the Prime Minister of the United Kingdom from May 1997 to June 2007. He was the first major head of government to bring climate change to the top of the international political agenda. He now works with world leaders on improving the world's environment.

 FACT **OR** **FICTION**

Freaky Fact or Fiction

139

The world's most wanted terrorist is on the US Federal Bureau of Investigation (FBI) list of the Ten Most Wanted. He is Osama bin Laden, leader of the organisation Al-Qaeda. Bin Laden is also sought by other nations for his terrorist activities. US intelligence officials say he is the prime suspect behind the September 11 hijacking attacks on American buildings. An Islamic fundamentalist, bin Laden was born in Saudia Arabia in 1957. He was the 17th of 54 children of a billionaire. The US State Department has offered a US$50 million (A$57.12 million or £30.35 million) reward for his arrest.

 ✓ FACT OR FICTION

140

Here's a world record for those of you who ride skateboards! In 2008, to the delight of a crowd of supporters, 13-year-old skating whizz Keith Baldassare broke the World Record for 'Most Consecutive Frontside Ollies on a Halfpipe'. Completing 348 ollies back-to-back, Keith achieved a longstanding personal best, and helped raise money for a local charity. Keith, of Florida, USA, has travelled throughout his country competing in skate contests and winning many first-place spots. Keith likes skating on cement, pools and mini-ramps.

✓ **FACT**   **OR**   **FICTION**

Freaky Fact or Fiction

141

The Horsehead Waterski Club from Tasmania, Australia, tried – and failed – seven times to break a world record. This record was for the most skiers towed behind a boat and remaining upright for 1 nautical mi (1.85 km or 1.15 mi). The previous record was set in Cairns, Australia, in 1986, with 100 skiers. On their eighth attempt in 2010, 114 skiers from the Horsehead club set off on Lake Barrington. They lasted the distance and set the new world record.

 ✓ **FACT** **OR** **FICTION**

142

For many years, people imagined what it would be like to land on and explore the Moon. In the 1960s, US President John F Kennedy decided that his country would succeed. On 20 July 1969, a man from the US said the historic words: 'One small step for man; one giant leap for mankind.' He was the Commander of the *Apollo 11* mission, Neil Armstrong, who became the first person to step onto the Moon's surface.

 ✓ FACT   **OR**   **FICTION**

143

Rusty MacTavish has won first prize in a quest to find Scotland's unluckiest man. Unfortunately, before he could accept his prize, Mr MacTavish was hit by a car driven by Lucy the Four-Legged Lady. Police have described it as a freak accident. Second prize went to Nigel McGurk, who holds the honour of being the only man to be struck by lightning in three consecutive years, and on the same day – his birthday. Mr McGurk won an all-expenses-paid trip to Glasgow, his home town.

✓ **FACT** **OR** **FICTION**

144

American Alia Sabur began talking and reading when she was only eight months old. She finished elementary school at age five and went to college when she was ten. By the time she was 14, Alia graduated top of her final year of a Bachelor of Science degree in applied mathematics. She was the youngest female in US history to do this. Then she earned a Master of Science and a PhD in materials science and engineering. When she was a few days short of her 19th birthday, Alia became the youngest person in 300 years to become a university professor, teaching in Seoul, Korea.

 ✓ **FACT**   **OR**   **FICTION**

145

The world's oldest building was discovered in 2000 by Japanese archeologists. They uncovered the remains of a shelter on a hillside north of Tokyo. It was built by an ancient human ancestor called *Homo erectus*, who used stone tools. The site is about half a million years old. It is made up of what look like ten post holes, forming two irregular pentagons. These could be the remains of two huts. Archeologists also found 30 stone tools on the site. Before this discovery, the oldest remains of a structure were in France. These were around 200,000 to 400,000 years old.

 ✓ **FACT** **OR** **FICTION**

146

The world's strangest bird is the Amazonian bulldog gummer. This rare bird is only found in one place: the muddy banks of Brazil's Lower Amazon. Fearful of predators, it uses its shovel-like beak to burrow deep into the mud. It then makes a nest, which it covers with twigs and leaves. Although it is small and timid, the bulldog gummer is renowned for its fighting ability when under attack. It has no teeth, but powerful suction pads on its gums enable it to hang on to its foe – like a bulldog.

✓ **FACT**   **OR**   **FICTION**

Freaky Fact or Fiction

147

The largest mud building in the world is the Great Mosque of Djenné in Mali, West Africa. The original mosque was built in the 13th century by an Islamic ruler, Sultan Kunburu. He built a mosque on the site to show how devoted he was to his new-found faith. The magnificent religious structure stood in the town for 600 years. The current mosque was completed in 1907 and its design is close to the original. The wooden 'spikes' on the outside walls actually support the mud bricks. It is forbidden for non-Muslims to enter the mosque.

 FACT **OR** **FICTION**

148

Country *Hitz* magazine has announced the winner of a competition to decide the saddest country song of all time. The winner is: 'You Threw My Heart on the Scrapheap of Love, and Now I'm Rusting Away, Babe'. To win the title, it had to beat off such tragic classics as 'I'll Love You Till There's No More Tomorrows – Even Though You Shot My Horse', and 'Hold My Hand as I Die and I Promise Not to Cry'.

 ✓ **FACT** **OR** **FICTION**

Freaky Fact or Fiction

149

The oldest living thing in the world is a tree. It is a bristlecone pine tree in the White Mountains of California, USA. Nicknamed 'Methuselah', the tree is over 4700 years old. Edmund Schulman, who worked in the Laboratory of Tree-Ring Research, explored the White Mountain trees in the 1950s and discovered the first tree that was over 4000 years old. He named it 'Pine Alpha'. In 1957, 'Methuselah' was found.

 ✓ **FACT** **OR** **FICTION**

150 In 1994, astronomers all around the world were excited when new planets were discovered in our universe. A radio astronomer, Alexander Wolszczan, reported what he called 'unambiguous proof' of planetary systems outside our solar system. Wolszczan had discovered a pulsar in the Virgo constellation that had two or three planet-sized objects orbiting it. (A pulsar is a dense, rapidly spinning leftover piece of a supernova explosion.) Scientists agree that these worlds couldn't support life as we know it. They would be harsh, barren places because of high-energy radiation.

 ✓ **FACT** OR **FICTION**

Freaky Fact or Fiction

151 Which are the oldest words in the English language? It's difficult to be 100 per cent sure. But evolutionary biologists at the University of Reading in the UK have identified some of the oldest words in the English language using computer analyses. They claim 'I', 'who', 'one', 'two' and 'three' are among the most ancient, dating back at least 10,000 years. The scientists say that adjectives like 'dirty' and verbs like 'squeeze' could disappear over the next eight centuries or so. This is because they aren't used as much as other words.

 FACT **OR** **FICTION**

152

For tennis lovers, here's a world record.

In 1877 the first Wimbledon Men's Tennis championship was held. There was a three-plank stand, which seated 30 spectators. Two hundred people attended the final. The tournament was held at the All England Club's first rented grounds on meadowland in the outer London suburb of Wimbledon. There were 22 entries and women were not allowed to play.

And the winner was 27-year-old W Spencer Gore.

✓ **FACT**   **OR**   **FICTION**

Freaky Fact or Fiction

153

General Nerdius Audacious Caesar, the youngest brother of Julius Caesar, is famous for making the worst military decision of all time. The bloodthirsty Platonic Hordes had destroyed everything in their path and were closing in on the biggest prize of all – Rome! Only Nerdius and his brave legions stood in their way. As he walked out to address his troops before the battle, Nerdius had what he thought was a brilliant idea. 'Change of tactics, boys,' he said. 'You can leave your swords at home today – we're going to stare them down!' It didn't work.

 ✓ **FACT** **OR** **FICTION**

154 Probably the most popular and best-known doll in the world is Barbie. American mother Ruth Handler noticed that her daughter Barbara liked giving her paper dolls grown-up roles when playing. She then found a doll in Germany called Bild Lilli, which was an adult rather than a baby doll. So Ruth, her husband and a business partner started a toy company called Mattel, which began producing Barbie in 1959. There have been 2000 different Barbie dolls, along with many dresses and accessories. There is even a Barbie fan club. Barbie's full name is Barbara Millicent Roberts.

✓ FACT OR FICTION

155

The undisputed yodelling champion of the world was the little Swiss master, Victor Scrumm. When he was just eight years old, he yodelled for Switzerland at the 1922 Alpine Games. He won three gold medals, as well as a silver in the relay, and a bronze in the hop, step and yodel. Scrumm soon proved he could yodel louder and longer than anyone. Over the next 13 years he was unbeatable, winning a total of 39 gold medals. His career ended in 1935, when, during a late night practice session, he was accidentally shot 22 times by a neighbour with a headache.

 ✓ **FACT** **OR** **FICTION**

156

Which is the world's oldest religion? Some people say Hinduism, some Zoroastrianism. At a remote site in the Ngamiland region of Botswana, Africans worshipped the python some 70,000 years ago. They also left more than 13,000 artefacts there, which were found much later by a Norwegian–Botswana team. These artefacts led archeologists to believe they had found the world's earliest religious worship site.

✓ **FACT** **OR** **FICTION**

Freaky Fact or Fiction

157 World records, especially in sport, keep being broken. But in 2009, Usain St Leo Bolt, a Jamaican sprinter and winner of three Olympic gold medals, became the first man to hold the 100-m and 200-m world and Olympic titles at the same time. At the 2008 Olympics in Beijing, China, Usain won three sprinting events. The last man to do this was American Carl Lewis in 1984. Bolt also became the first man to set world records in all three events at a single Olympics.

✓ FACT OR FICTION

158

One of the world's oldest known foods is bread. The oldest bread in Europe dates back to about 3700 BC. Prehistoric people made bread from grain flour (such as wheat, corn or rye) and water. In Egypt, around 1000 BC, bakers added yeast to make bread 'rise'. A new strain of wheat was also developed to make refined white bread. This was the first version of modern bread. Today there are many kinds of bread around the world including: naan (India), baguette (France), rye (Germany), bagel (Israel) and chappati (Pakistan).

✓ **FACT**   **OR**   **FICTION**

159

The first dog to go into orbit around the Earth was Bee-Jay, a Maltese terrier. Bee-Jay was aboard *Apollo 11* in 1969 when it made its famous Moon landing. A special canine spacesuit was made for the dog, with NASA (National Aeronautics and Space Administration) officials keen to see how animals adapted to space travel. Bee-Jay had no trouble with the Moon's atmosphere, but on the trip home one of the astronauts threw an apple core out of a window. Thinking it was a tennis ball, Bee-Jay followed it. Scientists believe he is still in orbit.

 ✓ **FACT**   **OR** **FICTION**

160

Do you enjoy playing with magnets? Imagine a magnet that can attract metal from 2.1 m (7 ft) away! The world's largest suspended electromagnet can be found in Ontario, Canada. Weighing 80 t (88 US t) – as much as 130 minivans – it was designed and built at the Walker Magnetics company. It was built to hang above a conveyor belt and pull iron and steel from ore flowing beneath. The Walker magnet is about 20 t (22 US t) bigger than the previous largest magnet.

 FACT OR **FICTION**

Freaky Fact or Fiction

161

Asia is the world's biggest continent. It covers 30 per cent of the world's total land area. It also has about 60 per cent of the world's people. One person in every five in the world lives in China. Africa is the second biggest continent but has the most countries, with 53.

 ✓ FACT OR FICTION

162

Many people believe that Uluru (also known as Ayer's Rock) in central Australia is the world's biggest rock. However, the world's biggest rock is Mt Augustus, in Western Australia, east of Carnarvon. Mt Augustus is two and a half times the size of Uluru, towering 717 m (2352 ft) above the surrounding stony, red sandplain. Its central ridge is almost 8 km (5 mi) long. The rock of Mt Augustus is about 1000 million years old. It sits on a granite rock that is believed to be about 1650 million years old.

✓ **FACT** **OR** **FICTION**

Freaky Fact or Fiction

163 In 2008, Spanish strongman El Toro Maximus set a new world record when he dragged a Boeing 747 (Jumbo Jet) 100 m (329 ft) in 74 seconds. Maximus had just stepped off the plane after a 22-hour flight. Because of a kitchen power failure, passengers had not eaten during the trip. By the time Maximus landed, the 175-kg (386-lb) giant was starving. As he made his way to a restaurant, a sudden breeze caused his scarf to be tangled in the plane's nose. Maximus just kept going. As he told reporters later, 'I was too hungry to stop.'

✓ **FACT** **OR** **FICTION**

World Records

The world's oldest burning coal fire is in Australia. Burning Mountain is near Wingen, New South Wales. Wingen takes its name from the word the indigenous Wanaruah people used for 'fire'. A naturally burning coal seam runs underground through the sandstone. Scientists estimate that the mountain has burned for 6000 years. European explorers and settlers in the area originally believed that the smoke was coming from a volcano. The fire is moving at a rate of about 1 m (3.3 ft) per year.

 ✓ FACT OR FICTION

Freaky Fact or Fiction

165 A fabulous world record breaker was the Portuguese adventurer, Ferdinand Magellan. At a time when people thought the Earth was flat, Ferdinand sailed as far as the eye could see – and further. He was the first man to lead an expedition round the world by sea. Near the end of his epic journey, Ferdinand and his crew ran out of food. They were forced to eat the leather that held the sails to the mast, as well as rats and sawdust. Ferdinand was killed in the Philippines, but two of his ships completed the journey in 1522.

 ✓ **FACT** **OR** **FICTION**

166

Jeans are the best-known pants in the western world. The word 'jeans' comes from a kind of material that was worn by Italian sailors. During the Californian gold rush in the US, the goldminers wanted clothes that were strong and durable. In 1853, a man called Leob Strauss (later known as Levi Strauss), made denim jeans for them to wear. Today, jeans are worn by men, women, boys and girls as working clothes or as a fashion item.

✓ **FACT** **OR** **FICTION**

Freaky Fact or Fiction

167 New Zealand is one of the most liberated countries in the world. In 1893, it became the first country in the world to make a law granting all of its women the right to vote in government elections. You can see the woman who led the campaign for the vote, Kate Sheppard, on New Zealand's $10 note. South Australian women were the first to gain the right to vote in Australia in 1894. But British and US women did not win the right to vote until after the first World War (1914–1918).

 FACT   **OR**   **FICTION**

168

The tiny country of Ruritania is famous as the bee-sting capital of the world. There are no more bees there than anywhere else, and the bees there aren't particularly vicious. So why are there so many bee stings? Well, it is because Ruritanians believe that beauty is in the eye of the bee holder. Wherever you go in Ruritania, you will see people grasping bees in their hands, and then looking at their eyes in a mirror! There is no evidence that this helps to make eyes beautiful, but it certainly makes the bees angry.

 ✓ FACT **OR** **FICTION**

169

The world's largest tuna, known as bluefish tuna, weigh up to 817 kg (1800 lb). Tuna migrate great distances to spawning and feeding grounds. In one instance, a fish tagged near California was caught in Japanese waters 10 months later. Tuna have a limited respiratory system. The current created when the fish swims ensures a flow of water over its gills, allowing it to breathe. If it stops swimming, it will die from lack of oxygen.

✓ **FACT** **OR** **FICTION**

170

In 1957, John Glenn became the first person to make a non-stop supersonic transcontinental flight, from Los Angeles to New York. His record  speed was 3 hours, 23 minutes, 8.4 seconds. In 1962, John became the first American to orbit the Earth in space, in the Project Mercury capsule *Friendship 7*. When he was 77, NASA sent John on another space mission. His task was to study the relationship between the effects of ageing and those of spaceflight on human bodily processes. He is the oldest person ever to go into orbit.

✓ **FACT**　　　**OR**　　　**FICTION**

171

The crested tiger owl is the fastest-selling domestic pet in Europe, even though it costs about US$500 (A$600 or £340). The crested tiger owl is great with children and other animals, and loves going for walks or a frolic at the beach. However, its popularity stems from the fact that it makes an excellent guard-bird. There is no need for a costly burglar alarm if you have a crested tiger owl. Being naturally protective, it stays awake all night to protect the house. If an intruder approaches the front door, the owl emits a terrifying growl that sounds like a hungry tiger.

 FACT **OR** **FICTION**

172

Manuel Diego Oleo is Spain's greatest living matador. For many years he had toiled away at his craft, but as late as 2002 he was rated only 77th on the list of the top 100 matadors. In 2003, he developed an allergy to bulls, which caused his nose to run and made him sneeze. Refusing to surrender, Oleo took to the bullring with a very large red handkerchief instead of a cape. The crowds loved this crazy fool with the soggy handkerchief! Soon Oleo was the greatest hero in Spain. They even gave him a new name: El Sneezo!

✓ FACT   OR   FICTION

173

Russian Yuri Gagarin was the first man to travel in space. In 1961, he was aboard the spaceship *Vostok 1* on a 27,400-km/h (17,026-mi/h) single orbit of the Earth. The flight lasted 1 hour, 48 minutes. The Russian success was the start of what is known as the Space Race between the US and Russia: an unofficial contest to see who would be first to conquer space. Gagarin died in a plane crash in 1968.

✓ **FACT** **OR** **FICTION**

174

What is said to be the world's most expensive painting doesn't have a descriptive title. It is also an abstract painting that looks more like scribbling than a traditional picture. It was painted by American Jackson Pollock and is titled 'No 5'. It sold at auction in 2006 for US$140 million (A$173 million or £97 million) to a Mexican multi-millionaire. The painting is huge at 2.4 m by 1.2 m (8 ft by 4 ft).

✓ FACT OR FICTION

175

The world's biggest baby is the blue whale calf. But the world's biggest human baby was a Canadian. According to Guinness World Records, the heaviest baby ever was born to Anna Bates in 1879. The baby weighed 10.8 kg (23.12 lb) but sadly died 11 hours after birth. The average human baby at birth weighs about one third that size. So baby Bates was certainly a giant!

✓ FACT OR FICTION

176 Nowadays many people give and receive greeting cards. The world's first commercial Christmas card was not made until 1843. It was designed by John Callcott Horsley and paid for by his friend Henry Cole, founder of the Victoria & Albert Museum. One thousand copies were published and they sold for one shilling each. The card is about the size of an ordinary postcard. It is made up of three parts. The middle shows a happy family gathering at a dinner table.

✓ FACT   OR   FICTION

Freaky Fact or Fiction ● ● ● ● ● ● ● ● ● ● ● ●

177

The world's luckiest person must surely be American Donna Goeppert. Mrs Goeppert won US$1 million (A$1.2 million or £690,000) in a lottery. That is certainly a lot of money. It allowed the 55-year-old grandmother to pay off her house and buy a new Cadillac. But then, just five months later, she won the same amount again in the same Pennsylvania game! The odds of hitting the jackpot once are 1.5 million to one. To do it twice, the odds rise to an amazing 419 million to one. Just how lucky is that?

 ✓ **FACT** **OR** **FICTION**

178

The world's first car race was held in 1887 in France – only then it wasn't known as car speed racing but 'wheel racing'. The race was organised by a Paris newspaper and ran 2 km (1.2 mi). It was won by Georges Bouton, who was the only competitor, in an electric car he had helped to build. The first drag race was also held in France, in 1897. Racing began soon after the first cars were made. Before that time, people raced in other vehicles such as horse-drawn buggies.

✓ **FACT** **OR** **FICTION**

The oldest woman in the world was Mrs Winifred Brown of Anchorage, Alaska, USA. Mrs Brown, who was born in 1872, was married five times and had 26 children and 214 grandchildren. She died by accident in 2006 at the age of 134. At the time of her death, Mrs Brown was helping her grandson, Jethro, change a flat tyre. Jethro had placed a bucket under the car wheel to support it while he got the spare tyre from the boot. While lying under the car, Mrs Brown accidentally kicked the bucket.

 FACT **OR** **FICTION**

180

The world's naughtiest children have to be Elsie Wright, 16, and her cousin Frances Griffiths, 11. In 1917, the two English girls played a trick that fooled the whole world for decades. Elsie took photos of Frances posing with fairies in a Cottingley garden. Many people believed that this was proof that fairies existed. However, in the early 1980s, Elsie and Frances admitted the truth. The 'fairies' were really cut-out drawings stuck to the ground with pins!

✓ **FACT** **OR** **FICTION**

Freaky Fact or Fiction

181

The world's longest wall is the Great Wall of China. Building the wall was a joint effort. Separate walls were first built between 476 and 221 BC by different kingdoms in China to protect their territories. Then the first Chinese Emperor, Qin Shihuang, decided to unify China, creating one Great Wall. It took more than one million people over 10 years to finish the work. The length was then over 6000 km (3728 mi) but much of the wall has now eroded. Some people say the wall can be seen from the Moon, but this is not true.

✓ **FACT** **OR** **FICTION**

182

He won the contest three times in a row (2003–2005) so Sam was the winner! Sam was the world's ugliest dog. And he was a purebred – a Chinese crested hairless dog. Sam won his world title in Santa Barbara, California, USA, where a county fair is held every year to find the ugliest mutt in the world. Sam was so ugly as a pup that he was put into a dog shelter. A kind woman found him there, took pity on him and gave him a home. Sadly, Sam died just before his 15th birthday in 2005.

 FACT **OR** **FICTION**

183

There have been many world champion chess players, but one of the greatest players of all time was Alexander Alekhine (1892–1946). The Russian player became one of the first chess grandmasters in 1914. He won the chess world championship in 1927 from a Cuban chess player and lost it to a Dutch chess player in 1935. He won the world title again in 1937 and maintained it until his death. Alexander was renowned for playing complex games in which he sacrificed his pieces to create attacking positions.

✓ **FACT** OR **FICTION**

184 The first victim of spontaneous combustion was Welsh inventor Fergus Bugnel. In his short life, Bugnel became known as one of the world's worst inventors. His efforts included an elephant detector and an underwater whistle to attract sharks. Both these inventions were commercial failures, but Bugnel tried again. In 1892, he invented the Spontaneous Combustion Stove. He tested it out by cooking two sausages. The stove became so hot that the sausages instantly exploded in flames and disappeared. And so did Bugnel.

✓ **FACT** **OR** **FICTION**

185

The America's Cup Race is said to be the world's top yacht race. Crews compete for the right to represent their home countries. The first contest for the prize, originally known as the Queen's Cup, was won by the yacht *America* in London in 1851. In 1857, the silver cup previously won by the *America* was presented to the New York Yacht Club to be held as a world perpetual trophy. After that it was known as the America's Cup. In 1983, *Australia II* defeated the United States entry, *Liberty,* for the first victory by a non-American boat in the race's history.

 ✓ **FACT** **OR** **FICTION**

186

A game that many families enjoy playing is the board game draughts. Also known as checkers, the game's object is to take as many of your opponent's pieces as possible, or make sure they cannot be moved. The game began in the 12th century in Europe, probably in the south of France. The first world championship for the game was awarded in 1847. Nowadays, computer programs, first developed in the 1950s, are stronger checkers players than humans. The current world champion draughts' player is Alexander Shvartsman of Russia.

 FACT **OR** **FICTION**

187

Many people love Enid Blyton's creation, Noddy. The cute little boy and his friends such as Big Ears, PC Plod, Tessie Bear and Bumpy Dog, live in Toy Town. In 1999, Betty and Johnny Hopton of Carmarthen, Wales, had the world's largest Noddy collection. Every room in their house had Noddy items – 1351 of them. Their most valuable Noddy item was a Noddy car, worth about US$1725 (A$2115 or £1195).

 ✓ **FACT** **OR** **FICTION**

188

What is the world's most common first name? It is often said that Muhammad (including the various spellings) is the most common given name in the world. Some estimates say that more than 15 million people in the world are called Muhammad. The most common surname (last name) in the world is Chang. In the UK in 2008, the most popular babies' names were Jack and Olivia. In the USA the most popular were Jacob and Emma. In Australia Jack and Ella topped the list.

 FACT OR FICTION

Freaky Fact or Fiction

189

Growing to 17 m (55.8 ft), the world's longest and rarest 'serpent' fish is the oarfish. It lives deep down in tropical and temperate marine waters. Believed to be the source of sea serpent myths, the thin, metallic silver oarfish is harmless. It feeds on plankton and fish. Usually it is only seen dead, washed up on the shore, or dying on the ocean's surface. But in 2010, scientists caught what is said to be the first deep-sea glimpse of this rare fish.

 ✓ **FACT** **OR** **FICTION**

190

Published in more than 2000 languages and dialects, the Bible is the world's best-selling book of all time. It is difficult to say exactly how many Bibles have been published and sold. The Bible Society believes the number printed between 1816 and 1975 was two billion, 458 million. A more recent survey (up to 1992) puts the number of Bibles sold at six billion. Other books that have been world best-sellers are *A Tale of Two Cities* by Charles Dickens and *The Lord of the Rings* by JRR Tolkien.

 FACT **OR** **FICTION**

Freaky Fact or Fiction

191

The world's best-selling diary was written by a teenage girl. *The Diary of Anne Frank*, which has sold more than 25 million copies, was written when Anne and her Jewish family were hiding from the Nazis during World War II. The best-selling children's book series is RL Stine's *Goosebumps* series. The 80 titles have sold 220 million copies worldwide. The highest one-year sales for a book series were the first three books in JK Rowling's *Harry Potter* series, which sold 23 million books in 1999.

 ✓ FACT OR FICTION

192

Have you ever wondered who wrote the best-selling children's books in the world? You might not know the names René Goscinny and Albert Uderzo, but it is likely you have read one of their 30 books about the comic-strip character Astérix the Gaul. Astérix books have sold some 250 million copies. Another comic-strip character whose books have sold at least 160 million copies is Tintin. Written by Belgian author–illustrator Georges Rémi (under the pen name Hergé), Tintin books have been translated into about 45 languages and dialects. Other best-selling children's authors include Enid Blyton, Dr Seuss, Beatrix Potter and Lewis Carroll.

 FACT **OR**   **FICTION**

Freaky Fact or Fiction

193

One of the world's greatest con men was Nigel Codswallip. In 1898, at the age of 17, he toured his mother across England in a show called *Betty the Bearded Lady*. Actually, his mother only had a small beard. Codswallip painted the rest on! A few years later he had a new show called *The Money Machine*. This starred his sister, Therese. With simple magician's tricks and clever lighting, Codswallip made it seem as if dollar bills actually grew out of Therese's body. No-one ever worked out his trick until he wrote his autobiography: *Money Doesn't Grow on Therese*.

 FACT **OR** **FICTION**

194

For a time, English novelist Charles Dickens held the world record for text messaging. Dickens, who said he liked to send text messages to help him relax after a hard day's writing, once texted fellow writers for 19 hours and 22 minutes without a break, shattering the previous world record set by Russian champion Fyodor Dostoevsky.

 ✓ **FACT** **OR**  **FICTION**

Freaky Fact or Fiction

195

The explosion of Krakatoa in Indonesia in 1883 was one of the biggest volcanic eruptions in recorded world history. It was 10,000 times more powerful than the atomic bomb blast that flattened the Japanese city of Hiroshima. It also affected the world's weather for five years and caused the Earth to cool. Ash fell over an area of 776,996 km^2 (300,000 mi^2) and the explosion could be heard 4828 km (3000 mi) away. Sadly, the explosion resulted in the deaths of 36,400 people.

 ✓ **FACT**   **OR**   **FICTION**

196

The world's most famous escape artist was Harry Houdini. Born Ehrich Weisz, Harry was handcuffed; bound with ropes, chains and straitjackets; locked in crates, boxes, steel trunks, prison cells and sealed coffins. He could escape them all. Once Harry was bound with chains, locked in a heavy trunk and dropped into a river. He was able to escape before he almost drowned. In the Chinese water torture cell act, he was chained upside down and submersed in water in a locked glass cell. It only took him a few minutes to escape. Harry died when someone punched him in the stomach while he had appendicitis.

 FACT **OR** **FICTION**

197

Norwegian adventurer Thor Heyerdahl believed ancient civilisations could have travelled to distant lands using primitive crafts. In 1947, he set out to prove his theory. With a six-man crew he sailed the Match-Stiki, a raft constructed entirely from matchsticks, across the Pacific Ocean, from Peru to Polynesia. The voyage took 101 days and covered 6980 km (4337 mi).

✓ FACT OR FICTION

198

Do you collect stamps? How many do you have? By the time he was 20, Jaishankar Prasad had collected stamps from more countries than any other Indian collector. When he was a boy, his English teacher asked Jaishankar's class to write letters. This is when his interest in stamps began. In 2008, he had collected stamps from 308 countries around the world.

 ✓ **FACT**   **OR**   **FICTION**

Freaky Fact or Fiction

199 In 1952, the World Hide-and-Seek Championships were held as part of the Helsinki Olympic Games. At the time, officials were considering whether to make hide-and-seek an official Olympic sport. However, they gave up on the idea when two of the contestants could not be found. In 1976, Hiram Smith was awarded a gold medal when he was eventually found hiding in a cupboard.

 ✓ FACT OR FICTION

200

Some have claimed to be younger, but certainly one of the youngest and most famous composers of all times was Wolfgang Amadeus Mozart. Born in 1756, Mozart is said to have started playing the keyboard at age three and composing minuets from the age of five. His production of *Apollo and Hyacinthus*, a musical in three acts, was performed when Mozart was just 11. Mozart composed over 600 works including operatic, piano and choral music.

✓ **FACT**   **OR**   **FICTION**

201

In 2010 in a world first, scientists made a dead person blink. US researchers used artificial muscles to make the eye blink when triggered by an electrical impulse. The artificial muscles are made from silicon. These can expand and contract in the same way that real muscles do. The use of artificial muscles could help people whose faces have been paralysed after a stroke or injury.

✓ **FACT** **OR** **FICTION**

202

Englishman David 'Tiny' Peters always wondered 'how long is a piece of string?'. In May 2008, he left his home in Birmingham on a quest to break a world record. In every country he went to, he asked people for pieces of string. Then he tied them together. By March 2010, Tiny had travelled to 15 countries and his string was 11,205 km (6962.5 mi) long. He now owns the world's longest piece of string!

 ✓ **FACT** **OR** **FICTION**

Freaky Fact or Fiction

203

The world's deadliest flower is the *Poisonia stonethrowa,* also known as cotoneaster. It produces seeds that contain a deadly poison called niacthin. Scientists estimate niacthin is 15,000 times more deadly than death-adder venom. It would take a tiny particle of niacthin to kill a 75-kg (165-lb) adult within five seconds. Only one person ever survived from eating cotoneaster – a witchdoctor from Nigeria where the plant is to be found.

✓ FACT OR FICTION

204 In 2010, a cure for brain disease came closer. For the first time, scientists were able to convert skin cells directly into brain cells. The result was nerve cells – or neurons – that could make connections with other nerve cells. Scientists used mice cells to make their amazing discovery. They said that if the same technique works with human cells, it could help in the treatment of brain and nerve diseases.

✓ FACT OR FICTION

Answers

• • • • • • • • • • • • • • • •

1. Fact.

2. Fact.

3. Fact.

4. Fact.

5. Fact.

6. **Fiction.**

7. Fact.

8. Fact.

9. Fact.

10. Fact.

11. Fact.

12. Fact.

13. **Fiction.** Patê is a food made from duck or goose liver, but the rest is untrue.

14. Fact.

15. Fact.

16. Fact.

17. Fact.

18. **Fiction.** Death by shark attack is actually quite uncommon.

19. Fact.

20. **Fiction.**

21. Fact.

22. Fact.

23. **Fiction.** The batfish does exist, but it is not a flying fish.

24. Fact.

25. Fact.

26. Fact.

27. **Fiction.**

28. Fact.

29. Fact.

30. Fact.

31. Fact.

32. Fact.

33. **Fiction.**

34. Fact.

35. Fact.

36. Fact.

37. **Fiction.**

38. Fact.

39. Fact.

40. Fact.

41. Fact.

42. Fact.

43. Fiction.

44. Fiction.

45. Fact.

46. Fact.

47. Fact.

48. Fact.

49. Fact.

50. Fact.

51. Fact.

52. Fiction. There is no tiny spotted whale. However, the pygmy sperm whale is one of the world's smallest whales.

53. Fact.

Answers

54. Fact.

55. Fact.

56. Fact.

57. Fact.

58. Fiction.

59. Fact.

60. Fact.

61. Fact.

62. Fact.

63. Fiction.

64. Fact.

65. Fact.

66. Fact.

67. Fiction.

68. Fact.

69. Fiction.

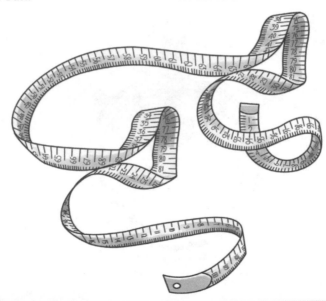

70. Fact.

71. Fact.

72. Fact.

73. Fact.

74. Fact.

75. Fact.

76. **Fiction.**

77. Fact.

78. Fact.

79. **Fiction.**

80. Fact.

81. Fact.

82. Fact.

83. Fact.

84. Fact.

85. Fact.

86. **Fiction.**

87. Fact.

88. Fact.

89. **Fiction.**

90. Fact.

91. Fact.

92. Fact.

93. **Fiction.**

94. Fact.

95. Fact.

96. Fact.

97. **Fiction.**

98. Fact.

99. Fact.

100. Fact.

101. **Fiction.**

102. Fact.

103. Fact.

104. Fact.

105. Fact.

106. **Fiction.**

107. Fact.

108. Fact.

109. Fact.

Answers

110. Fiction, though Shakespeare's *First Folio* was the most expensive book ever sold at auction in the UK.

111. Fact.

112. Fact.

113. Fact.

114. Fiction.

115. Fact.

116. Fact.

117. Fact.

118. Fact.

119. Fact.

120. Fiction.

121. Fact.

122. Fact.

123. Fact.

124. Fiction.

125. Fact.

126. Fact.

127. Fact.

128. Fact.

129. Fact.

130. Fact.

131. Fiction.

132. Fact.

133. Fact.

134. Fact.

135. Fact.

136. Fiction.

137. Fiction.

138. Fact.

139. Fact.

140. Fact.

141. Fact.

142. Fact.

143. Fiction.

144. Fact.

145. Fact.

146. Fiction.

147. Fact.

148. Fiction.

149. Fact.

150. Fact.

151. Fact.

152. Fact.

153. Fiction.

154. Fact.

155. Fiction.

156. Fact.

157. Fact.

158. Fact.

159. Fiction. The first dog – and the first living thing – to go into space was named Laika. She was launched into space aboard *Sputnik II* by the Russians in 1957, and orbited the Earth.

160. Fact.

Answers

161. Fact.

162. Fact.

163. **Fiction.**

164. Fact.

165. Fact.

166. Fact.

167. Fact.

168. **Fiction.**

169. Fact.

170. Fact.

171. **Fiction.**

172. **Fiction.**

173. Fact.

174. Fact.

175. Fact.

176. Fact.

177. Fact.

178. Fact.

179. **Fiction.**

180. Fact.

181. Fact.

182. Fact.

183. Fact.

184. **Fiction.** Spontaneous combustion is an extremely rare event where a body allegedly bursts into flames for no apparent reason. But this story is fictional!

185. Fact.

186. Fact.

187. Fact.

188. Fact.

189. Fact.

190. Fact.

191. Fact.

192. Fact.

193. **Fiction.**

194. **Fiction.** Text messaging, or SMS – Short Message Service – was first used in 1992, long after the deaths of Dickens (1812–1870) and fellow novelist Dostoevsky (1821–1881).

195. Fact.

196. Fact.

197. Fiction. The raft Heyerdahl used to cross the Pacific was constructed from balsa-wood logs. It was called the Kon-Tiki.

198. Fact.

199. Fiction.

200. Fact.

201. Fact.

202. Fiction.

203. Fiction. The real cotoneaster is a popular shrub or an annoying weed, depending on who you talk to. The berries are mildly poisonous, but it is not the world's deadliest flower.

204. Fact.

Sources

1. World Records Academy, www.worldrecordsacademy. org, 2008; 'Santa record bid attracts 13,000', BBC News, http://news.bbc.co.uk, 2007

2. Channel3000.com, www .channel3000.com, 2009; World Records Academy, www.worldrecordsacademy. org, 2009

3. National Geographic, http://animals. nationalgeographic.com, 2010; *Guinness World Records 2009* (book), 2009

4. *Scholastic Australian & World Records 2010* (book); TrekNature, www.treknature. com, 2007

5. *Guinness World Records 2009* (book), 2009; Government of South Australia, www .southaustralia.com, 2009; District Council of Coober Pedy, www.cooberpedy.sa .gov.au

6. Fiction.

7. *Reader's Digest Book of Facts*, 1986; National Geographic, http://kids. nationalgeographic.com, 2008; San Diego Zoo, www. sandiegozoo.org, 2010

8. *Scholastic Australian & World Records 2010* (book); NationMaster.com, www. nationmaster.com, 2010

9. *Guinness World Records 2009* (book), 2009; Encyclopaedia Britannica Online, www .britannica.com, 2010

10. Cedar Point, www.cedarpoint.com, 2010

11. The Eyes of Thailand, www.eyesofthailand.com, 2010; *Guinness World Records 2009* (book), 2009

12. *Scholastic Australian & World Records 2010* (book); 'World's 10 Largest Shopping Malls', Forbes, www.forbes. com, 2010

13. Fiction.

14. City Montessori School, www.cmseducation.org, 2010; Guinness World Records, www.guinnessworldrecords. com, 2010

15. *Guinness World Records 2010* (book), 2010

16. Ashrita Furman, www. ashrita.com, 2010; *Guinness World Records 2009* (book), 2009

17. Guinness World Records, www.guinnessworldrecords. com, 2010

18. Fiction.

19. Guinness World Records, www.guinnessworldrecords. com, 2010

20. Fiction.

21. 'A Rare Disorder: Stretchy Skin', abcNews.com, www. abcnews.go.com, 2007; Guinness World Records, www.guinnessworldrecords. com, 2010

22. The Tallest Man in the World, www. thetallestmanintheworld.com, 2010; Guinness World Records, www.guinnessworldrecords. com, 2010

23. Fiction.

24. Guinness World Records, www.guinnessworldrecords. com, 2010; 'Queen greeted by gurning champion', BBC News, www.bbc.co.uk, 2008; 'Tommy Mattinson wins world gurning title for 11th time', News & Star, www. newsandstar.co.uk, 2008

25. The Longest List of the Longest Stuff at the Longest Domain Name at Long Last, www.thelongestlistofthelongest stuffatthelongestdomainname atlonglast.com; Guinness World Records, www. guinnessworldrecords.com, 2010; Hand Research, www. handresearch.com, 2010

26. Guardian News and Media, www.guardian.co.uk, 2008; Woman's Day, www. womansday.ninemsn.com.au, 2007; Discovery Communications, www.tlc. discovery.com, 2010

27. Fiction.

28. Guinness World Records, www.guinnessworldrecords. com, 2010; Jackie 'The Texas Snake Man' Bibby, www. texsnakeman.com, 2009

29. YouTube, www.youtube. com, 2010 and 2008; The Internet Movie Database, www.imdb.com, 2010

30. *Scholastic Australian & World Records 2010* (book); Girl.com.au, www.girl.com.au, 2009

31. ESPN cricinfo, www. cricinfo.com, 2010

32. Australian Sports Commission, www.ausport. gov.au, 2010, e-bility.com, www.e-bility.com, 2005

33. Fiction.

34. *Scholastic Australian & World Records 2010* (book); The Skyscraper Picture website, www.skyscraperpicture.com, 2008

35. *Scholastic Australian & World Records 2008* (book); National Geographic, http:// animals.nationalgeographic. com, 2010

36. *Scholastic Australian & World Records 2010* (book); National Geographic, http:// animals.nationalgeographic. com, 2010

37. Fiction.

38. *Scholastic Australian & World Records 2010* (book); National Geographic, http:// animals.nationalgeographic. com, 2010

39. *Scholastic Australian & World Records 2010* (book); National Geographic, http:// animals.nationalgeographic. com, 2010

40. Bubblegum Heaven, www.bubblegumheaven.com, 2009; PR Leap, www.prleap. com, 2009

41. Chest of Books, http:// chestofbooks.com, 2009; *Ripley's Believe It or Not! Special Edition 2007* (book)

42. 'Malaysia's Scorpion Queen', BBC News, http:// news.bbc.co.uk, 2004; *Ripley's Believe It or Not! Special Edition 2007* (book)

43. Fiction.

44. Fiction.

45. *Scholastic Australian & World Records 2010* (book); AustralianFauna.com, www. australianfauna.com, 2006

46. *Scholastic Australian & World Records 2010* (book); Geology.com, www.geology. com, 2010

47. Guinness World Records, www.guinnessworldrecords. com, 2010; YouTube, www.youtube.com, 2007

48. *Scholastic Book of World Records 2010* (book); The Flower Expert, www. theflowerexpert.com, 2009

49. *Scholastic Australian & World Records 2008* (book); Transport Information Service (Germany), www. tis-gdv.de, 2010

50. '"Not too bright" thieves call bank in advance of robbery', Sydney Morning Herald, www.smh.com.au, 2010

51. 'The Cleanest Countries in the World', Forbes, www. forbes.com, 2010

52. Fiction.

53. *Scholastic Australian & World Records 2008* (book); Elvis Presley (official site), www.elvis.com, 2010

54. *Scholastic Australian & World Records 2008* (book); Ministry of Agriculture and Lands (British Columbia), www.agf.gov.bc.ca, 2007

Sources

55. *Scholastic Australian & World Records 2008* (book); Yahoo! Finance, www.finance.yahoo.com, 2009

56. *Scholastic Australian & World Records 2008* (book); Picasso Administration, www.picasso.fr, 2008

57. *Scholastic Australian & World Records 2010* (book); Forbes.com on MSNBC Digital Network, www.msnbc.msn.com, 2010; Oprah.com, www.oprah.com, 2008; Entrepreneur, www.entrepreneur.com, 2010

58. Fiction.

59. *Scholastic Australian & World Records 2008* (book); Forbes.com, www.forbes.com, 2003

60. *Scholastic Australian & World Records 2008* (book); Microsoft News Center, www.microsoft.com, 2010; Yahoo! Finance, www.finance.yahoo.com, 2010

61. *Scholastic Book of World Records 2009* (book); Forbes, www.forbes.com, 2007

62. *Scholastic Australian & World Records 2010* (book)

63. Fiction.

64. *Scholastic Australian & World Records 2008* (book); NASA, www.nasa.gov, 2007

65. The Official Shirley Temple website, www.shirleytemple.com; Bio.com, www.biography.com, 2007; The Internet Movie Database, www.imdb.com, 2010

66. '"Crabzilla": The biggest crab ever seen in Britain . . . and it's still growing', Mail Online, http://www.dailymail.co.uk, 2010; 'Man-sized Crab Shellshocks UK Crustacean Fans', HeraldSun.com.au, www.heraldsun.com.au, 2010

67. Fiction.

68. Guinness World Records, www.guinnessworldrecords.com, 2010; The Longest List of the Longest Stuff at the Longest Domain Name at Long Last, www.thelongestlistofthelongeststuffatthelongestdomainnameatlonglast.com

69. Fiction.

70. Guinness World Records, www.guinnessworldrecords.com, 2010

71. *Guinness World Records 2009* (book), 2009

72. *Guinness World Records 2010* (book), 2010; MySpace, www.myspace.com/burperking, 2010

73. *Guinness World Records 2009* (book), 2009; YouTube, www.youtube.com, 2009

74. *Guinness World Records 2009* (book), 2009

75. 'We're 205 Years Old', The Sun, www.thesun.co.uk, 2008; 'With a Combined Age of 205, Meet Britain's Oldest Couple', Mail Online, www.dailymail.co.uk, 2008

76. Fiction.

77. www.CharinsDream.com, www.charinsdream.com, 2009; Guinness World Records, www.guinnessworldrecords.com, 2010

78. Guinness World Records, http://community.guinnessworldrecords.com, 2009; Miami Dade College, www.mdc.edu, 2010

79. Fiction.

80. *Guinness World Records 2008* (book), 2008; 'Pacific Ocean', The World Almanac for Kids, www.worldalmanacforkids.com, 2010; Guy Campbell and Mark Devins, *The World's Most Amazing Planet Earth Facts for Kids* (book), 2002

81. *Guinness World Records 2008* (book), 2008; 'Branson, Gore Announce 25 million "Virgin Earth Challenge"', Environmental Leader, www.environmentalleader.com, 2007

82. *Guinness World Records 2008* (book), 2008; The Physics Factbook, www.hypertextbook.com, 2002

83. Penguin Facts, www.penguinfacts.net, 2007; Penguins for Kids, www.penguins-world.com, 2009; National Geographic, http://animals.nationalgeographic.com, 2010; *Guinness World Records 2008* (book), 2008

84. *Guinness World Records 2008* (book), 2008; Arizona-Sonora Desert Museum, www.desertmuseum.org, 2008

85. The Most Expensive Journal, http://most-expensive.net, 2006; Neatorama, www.neatorama.com, 2007

86. Fiction.

87. *Guinness World Records 2008* (book), 2008; National Geographic, http://animals.nationalgeographic.com, 2010

88. *Guinness World Records 2008* (book), 2008; National Geographic, http://news.nationalgeographic.com, 2006; Perth Zoo, www.perthzoo.wa.gov.au, 2009

89. Fiction.

90. BBC Science & Nature, www.bbc.co.uk, 2008

91. David M Bird, *The Bird Almanac: A Guide to Essential Facts and Figures of the World's Birds* (book), 2004; National Geographic, http://animals.nationalgeographic.com, 2010

92. National Geographic, http://channel.nationalgeographic.com, 2010; *Guinness World Records 2008* (book), 2008

93. Fiction.

94. 'Giant African Land Snails Fact Sheet', Official State of Michigan website, www.michigan.gov, 2004; 'Giant Snails, Once a Delicacy, Overrun Brazil', National Geographic News, http://news.nationalgeographic.com, 2007; *Guinness World Records 2008* (book), 2008

95. *Guinness World Records 2008* (book), 2008; National Geographic, http://animals.nationalgeographic.com, 2010

96. *Guinness World Records 2008* (book), 2008; National Geographic, http://animals.nationalgeographic.com, 2010

97. Fiction.

98. National Geographic, http://animals.nationalgeographic.com, 2010; Guy Campbell and Mark Devins, *The World's Most Amazing Planet Earth Facts for Kids* (book), 2002; Australian Museum, http://australianmuseum.net.au, 2010; How Stuff Works, http://animals.howstuffworks.com, 2010

Sources

99. Encyclopaedia Britannica Online, www.britannica.com, 2010; 'Tallest Mountains in the World: The Highest Peaks on Planet Earth', Matt Rosenberg, About.com, http://geography.about.com, 2010

100. 'UK Backs Chagos Islands Marine Reserve', The Sydney Morning Herald, http://news.smh.com.au; 'UK Sets Up Chagos Islands Marine Reserve', BBC News, http://news.bbc.co.uk, 2010

101. Fiction.

102. 'Woman Guilty of Swapping Children for $195 and a Cockatoo', The Sydney Morning Herald, http://www.smh.com.au, 2010

103. *Guinness World Records 2008* (book), 2008; AlainRobert.com, http://www.alainrobert.com/index.php/english/TRIVIA.html, 2009

104. The Official Website of Denmark, The Ministry of Foreign Affairs of Denmark, www.denmark.dk, 2009; Guy Campbell and Mark Devins, *The World's Most Amazing Planet Earth Facts for Kids* (book), 2002

105. Guy Campbell and Mark Devins, *The World's Most Amazing Planet Earth Facts for Kids* (book), 2002; An Introduction [of] Chinese Words, www.ingo.com, 2008; How to Learn Any Language, http://how-to-learn-any-language.com, 2009

106. Fiction.

107. Guy Campbell and Mark Devins, *The World's Most Amazing Planet Earth Facts for Kids* (book), 2002; 'The London Underground', Jackie Craven, About.com, www.architecture.about.com, 2010

108. Guy Campbell and Mark Devins, *The World's Most Amazing Planet Earth Facts for Kids* (book), 2002; 'China Population: The Population Growth of the World's Largest Country', Matt Rosenberg, About.com, http://geography.about.com, 2008

109. Stumblerz, www.stumblerz.com, 2008; Hairy Human, www.hairyhuman.co.uk, 2005; *Guinness World Records 2008* (book), 2008

110. Fiction.

111. *Guinness World Records 2008* (book), 2008; 'World's First "Bionic Woman"', Med Gadget: Internet Journal of Medical Technologies, www.medgadget.com, 2006

112. Central Intelligence Agency, www.cia.gov, 2010

113. Unexplained-Mysteries.com, www.unexplained-mysteries.com, 2006; The Longest List of the Longest Stuff at the Longest Domain Name at Long Last, http://thelongestlistofthelongeststuffatthelongestdomainnameatlonglast.com; *Guinness World Records 2008* (book), 2008

114. Fiction.

115. World Database of Happiness, www.worlddatabaseofhappiness.eur.nl, 2009

116. *Guinness World Records 2008* (book), 2008; One India, http://living.oneindia.in, 2007

117. *Guinness World Records 2009* (book), 2009; Mount Everest History and Facts, www.mnteverest.net, 2001

118. *Guinness World Records 2008* (book), 2008; Beyond the Invisible, http://bethei. blogspot.com, 2007

119. *Guinness World Records 2008* (book), 2008; 'Boy Born with Heart Outside His Body Defies Odds', ABC News, http://abcnews.go.com, 2009

120. Fiction.

121. KSL Broadcasting Salt Lake City Utah, www.ksl. com, 2009; '43 Snails On Boy's Face For World Record', The Huffington Post, www.huffingtonpost.com, 2009

122. *Guinness World Records 2008* (book), 2008; 'Eco-friendly Francis Joyon takes fortnight off Dame Ellen MacArthur's world record', *The Times* (newspaper), www. timesonline.co.uk, 2008

123. Steve Fossett Challenges, www.stevefossett. com, 2006; Social Studies for Kids, www.socialstudiesfor kids.com, 2002

124. Fiction.

125. *Guinness World Records 2010* (book), 2010; 'Man Breaks Underwater Cycling Record', Telegraph.co.uk, www.telegraph.co.uk, 2008

126. 'Obama, aka Fat Little Barry Remembered', The Sydney Morning Herald, www.smh.com.au, 2008; Barack Obama, *The Audacity of Hope* (book), 2006

127. 'Cypress Gardens Hosts "World's Largest Easter Egg Hunt"', Sys-con Media, http:// search.sys-con.com, 2007; *Guinness World Records 2008* (book), 2008

128. *Guinness World Records 2008* (book), 2008; *Guinness World Records 2009* (book) 2009; 'Vegetable Growers Rejoice In Wet Summer', Telegraph.co.uk, www. telegraph.co.uk, 2008

129. *Guinness World Records 2010* (book), 2010; Front Range Frenzy, www. frontrangefrenzy.com, 2009; 'The World's Tallest Horse Meets the World's Smallest', Mail Online, www.dailymail. co.uk, 2007

130. 'UK Rock Beats US Scissors', BBC One-Minute World News, http://news.bbc. co.uk, 2006; 'Hundreds Compete for Rock, Paper, Scissors Title', USA Today, www.usatoday.com, 2006; 'Rock Paper Scissors World Championships', Sportz Fun, sportzfun.com, 2010

131. Fiction.

132. *Guinness World Records 2008* (book), 2008; Cool Furries, www.coolfurries.com, 2010

133. Kumbha Mela, www. kumbhamela.net, 2010; *Guinness World Records 2008* (book), 2008

134. *Guinness World Records 2008* (book), 2008; Swiss National Bank, www.snb.ch, 2010

135. TV.com, CBS Entertainment, www.tv.com, 2010; Hollywood Remains to Be Seen, www.cemeteryguide. com, 2010; *Guinness World Records 2008* (book), 2008

136. Fiction.

137. Fiction.

138. 'Long Serving Prime Ministers', BBC One-Minute World News, http://news.bbc. co.uk, 2003; The Office of Tony Blair, www. tonyblairoffice.org, 2010; *Guinness World Records 2008* (book), 2008

139. 'Bin Laden, Millionaire with a Dangerous Grudge', CNN.com, http://archives.cnn. com, 2001; *Guinness World Records 2010* (book), 2010

Sources

140. The Beachside Resident, http://thebeachsideresident.com, 2008; Central Florida News 13, www.cfnews13.com, 2008

141. 'Water Ski Record, Finally', *The Mercury* (newspaper), Tasmania, Australia, 29 March 2010; Channel 7 News (television), Australia, 30 March 2010

142. NASA, www.nasa.gov, 2007; Kidport Reference Library, www.kidport.com, 2010; Brian Williams, *The Greatest Book of the Biggest and Best* (book), 2001

143. Fiction.

144. 'World's Youngest Professor Can't Legally Drink', Today at MSNBC.com, http://today.msnbc.msn.com, 2008; YouTube, www.youtube.com, 2008

145. 'World's Oldest Building Discovered', BBC News, http://news.bbc.co.uk, 2010

146. Fiction.

147. Pilot Destinations, www.pilotguides.com, 2008; Brian Williams, *The Greatest Book of the Biggest and Best* (book), 2001; UNESCO World Heritage, http://whc.unesco.org, 2009; Annenberg Media, www.learner.org, 2010

148. Fiction.

149. The Ancient Bristlecone Pine, www.sonic.net, 2005; US Forest Service, www.fs.fed.us, 2009 and 2007

150. HistoryOrb.com, www.historyorb.com, 2010; Planet Quest, NASA, http://planetquest.jpl.nasa.gov

151. 'Supercomputer Finds Oldest English Words', ABC Science, www.abc.net.au, 2009; Neatorama, www.neatorama.com, 2009

152. Wimbledon: The Official Website, www.wimbledon.org, 2010; Tennis Theme, www.tennistheme.com, 2009

153. Fiction.

154. Brian Williams, *The Greatest Book of the Biggest and Best* (book), 2001; Barbie Collector, www.barbiecollector.com, 2010

155. Fiction.

156. 'World's Oldest Religion Discovered in Botswana', Afrol News, www.afrol.com, 2010; Hinduism: The World's Oldest Religion, http://afgen.com, 2004; ReligiousTolerance.org, www.religioustolerance.org, 2008

157. Olympic.org: Official Website of the Olympic Movement, www.olympic.org, 2009; Usain Bolt Fan Site, www.usainbolt.co.uk, 2010; Squidoo, www.squidoo.com, 2010; Government of Jamaica, Jamaica Information Service, www.jis.gov.jm, 2010

158. Breadinfo.com, www.breadinfo.com, 2010; All Empires, www.allempires.com, 2007; Mueller Science, www.muellerscience.com, 2010

159. Fiction.

160. Walker Magnetics, http://walkermagnet.com, 2010

161. Brian Williams, *The Greatest Book of the Biggest and Best* (book), 2001; 'China Population: The Population Growth of the World's Largest Country', Matt Rosenberg, About.com, http://geography.about.com, 2010

162. Department of Environment and Conservation, Government of Western Australia, www.dec.wa.gov.au, 2010; 'Mt Augustus: World's Biggest Rock', Larry Rivera, About.com, http://goaustralia.about.com, 2010

163. Fiction.

164. Guy Campbell and Mark Devins, *The World's Most Amazing Planet Earth Facts for Kids* (book), 2002; Google Earth Hacks, www. gearthhacks.com, 2007; 'Burning Mountain – Places to See', The Sydney Morning Herald Online, www.smh. com.au, 2010

165. Guy Campbell and Mark Devins, *The World's Most Amazing Planet Earth Facts for Kids* (book), 2002; Answers.com Reference Answers, www.answers.com/ topic/ferdinand-magellan, 2010

166. Brian Williams, *The Greatest Book of the Biggest and Best* (book), 2001; New Internationalist: Global Issues for Learners of English, www.newint.org, 1999

167. New Zealand History Online, www.nzhistory.net. nz, 2009; Guy Campbell and Mark Devins, *The World's Most Amazing Planet Earth Facts for Kids* (book), 2002; Parliament of New South Wales, www.parliament.nsw. gov.au, 2009; Scholastic: Teachers, http://teacher. scholastic.com, 2010

168. Fiction.

169. *Encarta Encyclopedia* (CD), 1999

170. *Encarta Encyclopedia* (CD), 1999; NASA, www.jsc.nasa.gov, 1999

171. Fiction.

172. Fiction.

173. *Encarta Encyclopedia* (CD), 1999 *National Geographic* (book), 1965; 'Yuri Gagarin' NASA, http:// starchild.gsfc.nasa.gov, 2009

174. 'Top 10: World's Most Expensive Paintings', HubPages, http://hubpages. com, 2010; 'The 15 Most Expensive Paintings in the World', StyleCrave, http:// stylecrave.com, 2008; The Department of Music at Columbia University, http:// music.columbia.edu, 2009

175. *Guinness World Records 2008* (book), 2008; *Guinness World Records 2010* (book), 2010; 'Woman Gives Birth to "Giant Baby"', BBC News, http://news.bbc.co.uk, 2005

176. The British Postal Museum & Archive, http:// postalheritage.org.uk, 2010; The Scrap Album, www. scrapalbum.com, 2009

177. 'Lottery Double Shocks US Granny', BBC News, http://news.bbc.co.uk, 2005; *Ripley's Believe It or Not! Special Edition* 2007 (book), 2007; 'Lady Luck Hits Jackpot Twice', CBS News, www.cbsnews.com, 2005

178. Did You Know It, www. didyouknow.it, 2010, *Ripley's Believe It or Not! Special Edition 2007* (book), 2007

179. Fiction.

180. The Haunted Museum, www.prairieghosts.com.html, 2008; Answers.com Reference Answers, www.answers.com, 2010; *Ripley's Believe It or Not! Special Edition 2007* (book), 2007

181. China Highlights, www. chinahighlights.com, 2009; Brian Williams, *The Greatest Book of the Biggest and Best* (book), 2001; Robert Dolezal, *Reader's Digest Book of Facts* (book), 1987; China National Tourist Office, www.cnto.org, 2010

182. *Ripley's Believe It or Not! Special Edition 2007* (book), 2007, The Ugliest Dog!, www.samugliestdog. com, 2008; Sam – 'World's Ugliest Dog', www. samugliestdogever.com, 2006

Sources

183. *Encarta Encyclopedia* (CD), 1999; Chess Corner, www.chesscorner.com, 2010

184. Fiction.

185. *Encarta Encyclopedia* (CD), 1999; 34th America's Cup, www.americascup.com, 2010

186. *Encarta Encyclopedia* (CD), 1999; 'World Champion Alexander Shvartsman: "Draughts is Sport"', Draughts, www.wmsg-draughts.org, 2008

187. Guinness World Records, www.guinnessworldrecords.com, 2010; The Longest List of the Longest Stuff at the Longest Domain Name at Long Last, http://thelongestlistofthelongeststuffatthelongestdomainnameatlonglast.com; The Enid Blyton Society, www.enidblytonsociety.co.uk, 2010

188. Office for National Statistics, www.statistics.gov.uk, 2009; 'Muhammad is Number 2 in Boy's Names', Times Online, 2007; Behind the Name, www.behindthename.com, 2010; CNN.com/living, http://edition.cnn.com, 2009; McCrindle Research, www.mccrindle.com.au, 2009

189. 'Deep Sea Thrill: "Serpent" of Myths Filmed', The Sydney Morning Herald online, www.smh.com.au, 2010

190. Buzzle.com, www.buzzle.com, 2010; ipl2, www.ipl.org, 2008

191. Buzzle.com, www.buzzle.com, 2010; ipl2, www.ipl.org, 2008; Anne Frank House, www.annefrank.org, 2010

192. Buzzle.com, www.buzzle.com, 2010; ipl2, www.ipl.org.html, 2008

193. Fiction.

194. Fiction.

195. 'Volcanoes', *History Magazine* (magazine), Canada, October/November 2001; Encyclopaedia Britannica Online, www.britannica.com, 2010

196. Appleton Public Library, www.apl.org, 2004; American Experience: Public Broadcasting Service, www.pbs.org, 1999; Essortment, www.essortment.com, 2002

197. Fiction.

198. World Amazing Records (India), www.worldamazingrecords.com, 2009

199. Fiction.

200. 'World's Youngest Composers', Sunday Observer, www.sundayobserver.lk, 2010; California Institute of Technology: Music Courses, www.its.caltech.edu, 1996

201. 'Dead Man Winking: Discovery Offers Hope to Paralysis Victims', *The Sydney Morning Herald* (newspaper), Sydney, Australia, 20 January 2010

202. Fiction.

203. Fiction.

204. 'Cure for Brain Diseases Closer as Adult Skin Cells Turned into Nerves', *The Sydney Morning Herald* (newspaper), Sydney, Australia, 28 January 2010